PHILOSOPHICAL STANDARDISM

PHILOSOPHICAL STANDARDISM

AN EMPIRICIST APPROACH TO PHILOSOPHICAL METHODOLOGY

NICHOLAS RESCHER

UNIVERSITY OF PITTSBURGH PRESS

PITTSBURGH AND LONDON

Published by the University of Pittsburgh Press,
Pittsburgh, Pa. 15260

Manufactured in the United States of America
Printed on acid-free paper

Library of Congress Cataloging-in-Publication Data

Rescher, Nicholas.
Philosophical standardism : an empiricist approach to philosophical methodology / Nicholas Rescher.
p. cm.
Includes bibliographical references and index.
ISBN 0-8229-3790-5 (alk. paper)
1. Methodology. 2. Empiricism. 3. Norm (Philosophy) 4. Truth. 5. Inconsistency (Logic) I. Title.
BD241.R443 1994
101—dc20 93-46836
CIP

A CIP catalogue record for this book is available from the British Library.
Eurospan, London.

To four philosopher friends in Italy:

Alejandro Agazzi
Andrea Bottani
Diego Marconi
Michele Marsonet

CONTENTS

PREFACE

THIS LITTLE BOOK on philosophical method was drafted during a brief visit in Mainz, Germany, in April of 1990, on the occasion of my participation in a Kant Congress. It was largely written in Oxford during the summer of 1990 and refined and polished in Pittsburgh during 1990–1992. Its distinctly non-Kantian deliberations represent a confluence of lines of thought that had been stirring in my mind for several years.

I am indebted to Marian Kowatch and Annamarie Morrow for their patient help in having the manuscript take form on the word processor through the course of numerous revisions. I am most grateful to Annette Baier, Jon Mandle, Katarzyne Paprzycka, and several anonymous publisher's readers for reading earlier versions of the book and enabling me to profit from their constructive comments.

Pittsburgh, Pa.
June 1992

PHILOSOPHICAL STANDARDISM

INTRODUCTION

THE OBJECT of the book is to propound an unorthodox approach to philosophical doctrines that is predicated on the idea of *standardism*, namely, the policy of interpreting the generalizations of the field not as making their claims *universalistically* (i.e., exceptionlessly), but rather as making them *standardistically*, that is, as stating how matters stand "normally" or "as a rule." (Such generalizations are not to be confused with merely statistical generalizations such as "Most but not all *X*s are *Y*s.") Such a standardistic approach to its generalizations abandons the necessitarian pretentions of traditional philosophizing in favor of a more modest and cautious perspective that looks to what our experience of the world indicates to be its normal course of things. The enterprise now assumes a far more tentative and empirical demeanor than has been its traditional wont, gearing our understanding of the world to its experienced realities rather than to supposedly abstract necessities of general principle.

Standardism accordingly proposes to construe philosophical generalizations in terms of limited rather than strict universality, looking to what is ordinarily and normally the case rather than to what is unexceptionally and necessarily the case. Such qualified generalizations can function effectively in explanatory contexts subject to an assumption of normal circumstances. In consequence, our philosophical explanations become geared to the normal course of things as our experience reveals it, and this "empirical" aspect plays a key role in the rational reconceptualization of the field. In particular, standardism sees our philosophical explanations as based on limited generalizations that are subject to revision in the light of future evidence. The price one pays for this modest and less demanding construal of philosophical generalizations is to acknowledge the essential openendedness of our philosophically relevant concepts and the porous and fragile make-up of the claims that we can appropriately stake in terms of them. By way of compensation, however, this policy provides us with a way of resolving a whole host of philosophical problems (such as the Gettier problem) that have lingered too long because of the mistaken but pervasive belief that philosophical generalizations will be adequate only if they do not admit of exception in any contexts.

What recommends philosophical standardism is the experientially manifested infeasibility of finding any generalizations regarding the important issues of philosophy that are at once nontrivial and exceptionlessly true. In this philosophical domain we cannot conjointly achieve in high degree both tenability and precision. If we do not want to leave the philosophical arena virtually empty-handed, we would therefore do well to settle for a more modest empirical approach that abandons the absolutistic aspirations of traditional philosophizing. After all, the focal concepts of our philosophizing—concepts that figure in the propositions whose formulation and elucidation constitute the very fabric of philosophy and provide its reason for being—are inextricably rooted in the reach of our experience—in the *empirical* world. Philosophy's traditional quest for aprioristic absolutes rests on an unrealizable illusion.

Philosophy is accordingly led to take an empirical turn and to address itself to the world's realities as we find them within the orbit of our experience (broadly construed to examine *intellectual* experience as well). The philosopher's ancient dream of resolving the questions of the field a priori, on the basis of abstract general principles that obtain with universality and necessity, will have to be abandoned. ("And about time, too!" says the standardist.)

In its endeavor to validate this deflated standardistic approach to philosophy, the book will offer a variety of detailed case studies that show its advantages in averting or resolving various otherwise perplexing issues in epistemology, ethics, metaphysics, and metaphilosophy. Its position is accordingly defended not just by presenting theoretical considerations, but also by exhibiting concrete examples of standardism's instrumental advantages in handling particular philosophical issues.

ONE

How Standardism Works

SYNOPSIS

(1) Standardism proposes to construe generalizations in terms of a limited *rather than* strict *universality. Its approach is to focus upon what happens* normally *and as a rule, rather than address what happens* invariably *and exceptionlessly. (2) Even such standardistically construed generalizations are able to meet the demands of explanatory employment—though, clearly, this employment always has to be predicated on a* presumption of normalcy. *Such a focus upon the normal, ordinary course of things that contents itself with theses geared to how things stand generally and as a rule (rather than universally and necessarily) makes a standardistic approach into an indelibly empirical enterprise. For the normal and customary is and has to be defined relative to a pattern of occurrence within a course of experience. (3) Philosophical standardism is the doctrinal position of insisting on a standardistic approach to philosophical generalizations. But why should we settle for this more modest and less demanding view of the philosophical enterprise?*

1. The Standardistic Approach to Generalizations

To be viable, contentions in everyday discourse will ordinarily have to be framed as *provisoed* assertions. They will generally be subject to implicit qualifications and reservations that relate to what happens *customarily* or *ordinarily* or *standardly* or *other things being equal* (ceteris paribus) or the like. We often say things like "humans can reason" or "birds can fly," realizing full well that the claim as it stands is inaccurate and imprecise, which is to say strictly incorrect. In ordinary life we get by with saying how things run *normally* or *as a rule* because our interlocutors can in general supply the needed qualifications. Everyday-life generalizations are secured against remote spoiling possibilities through the fact that we do not intend them to be taken rigorously and unrestrictedly, without being accorded any "benefit of qualification." As with the precept "Never say never," we do not want them to be construed with inflexible literalness.

A general statement of the form "*A*s are (are not) *B*s" admits of two alternative constructions. One is the *universalistic* reading, "Invariably and exceptionlessly, all/no *A*s and *B*s." The other is the *standardistic* reading, "Standardly and ordinarily, *A*s are (are not) *B*s." To say the latter is tantamount to saying that *A*s are (are not) *B*s *as a rule*, recognizing that this rule, like most, may admit of exceptions.

On this sort of reading, statements of a general form are to be construed not with *strict* universality, but in a *permeably* universal way of a qualified generalization that states merely how matters stand normally, standardly, and "in the usual course of things." So taken, the acceptability of standardistic generalizations is not at odds with the recognition of exceptions of various kinds. The generality of standardistically construed generalizations is an imperfect one: They are not literally and strictly universal, but are subject to a qualification on the lines of standardly/customarily/as a rule as opposed to holding always/invariably/exceptionlessly.

Standardistic generalizations are tailor-made for the articulation of certain kinds of social regularities (as contrasted with natural laws). Instances abound in human affairs, where, for example, we have

- Americans who earn more pay higher income taxes.
- People who take good care of their health live longer lives.

The exception categories in the first instance include, for example, investors in tax-free securities, tax shelters, and high-deduction taxpayers (with large families, extensive medical expenses, and so on). In the second case, the exceptions are people with genetically based health problems, accident victims, and so on. Standardistic generalizations are not, however, confined to human affairs. Thus consider "snowflakes fall downward." This is certainly true in general, but exceptions can occasionally arise due to wind currents, updrafts, and the like.

Let us stress that "Standardly, *A*s are *B*s" is *not* tantamount to "*A*s are mostly (majoritatively, almost always) *B*s." Holding *standardly* is not simply a matter of "mostly yes, sometimes no," with the exceptional cases lost from sight—and comprehension—in a statistical fog. These standardized (rather than universalized) generalizations look to what is the norm or rule—to what happens normally and ordinarily, and thus not merely to what happens usually or predominantly. And the exceptions must, as a rule, fall into recognizable categories, since these abnormal cases must in principle be identifiable as such. With standardism, exceptions are a matter of identifiable and explicable failures to conform to well-defined rules: They must belong to a context-coordinated natural kind in this regard. It would thus be perfectly correct to say "Standardly, English sentences contain a verb," because the exceptions to that general rule (including such exclamations as "Oh no! Not rain again!") belong to categories specifiable independently of their simply being exceptions to the generalization at issue. However, note that this would *not* be the case for

- Standardly, days of the year are not days in January.
- Standardly, Americans like ice cream.

While such statements would qualify as true if taken in a merely statistical sense, they are in fact inappropriate (i.e., not unproblematically correct) taken standardistically, because there is no meaningful, noncircular way of categorizing the exceptions and of "explaining them away."

For standardism, the crux is not just that there are exceptions but that we can account for them in the sense of providing a cogent, noncircular explanation for how and why it is that these exceptions are qualified as such, for standardized generalizations can generally be reconstrued universalistically:

> *A*s are always/never *B*s save for cases belonging to various categories of exceptions for whose nonconformity there is a cogent explanation.

Someone who asserts "American newspapers are published in English" in its standardistic vein should thus be in a position to explain why this is not the case with *El Diario* of Miami, and can discharge this obligation by noting that this daily is aimed at the Hispanic clientele of a city with an extensive population of Latin American refugees. (Note, however, that we may or may not be able to inventory all of those exception categories in advance.)

The distinction between the standardistic situation and the statistical is reflected in the following categorization of cognate locutions:

STATISTICAL	NEUTRAL	STANDARDISTIC
predominantly	generally	standardly
usually	in general	ordinarily
commonly	typically	as a rule
by and large		normally
virtually always		customarily

Even as there is more to an actual law than there is to a merely accidental universal relationship, so there is more to a genuinely standardistic linkage than to a merely statistical correlation regarding what happens to be the case predominantly and for the most part. (To say that a standardistic generalization is not merely statistical in its meaning content is not, of course, to deny that statistical evidence can be one positive factor in its epistemic support.) Statistical relationships are *purely* extensional; standardistic ones are not because exception explicability introduces an ineliminable element of nonextensionality. In standardistic generalizations, a normative, rulish aspect is absent in the statistical case; as the very name suggests, standardism involves a normative orientation that pivots matters on the operation of *standards* or *rules* of some sort. By contrast "generally" and "in general" may be seen as neutral because a generalization can in principle be construed in either the statistical or the standardistic sense. The crux is that statistical generalizations are *merely* that—simply and purely matters of counting. Standardistic generalizations on the other hand do not shrug off exceptions as "just one of those things" but extend an implicit guarantee of their explicability. (In the social sciences the difference shows in the distinction between *standards* from which the exceptions fall off in categorizable ways and *stereotypes* whose exceptions are simply as matters of gratuitous chance.)

In this regard the *normal* is significantly different from the *typical*. Normalcy is a matter of conformity (or lack thereof) to a natural kind of some sort. But being a typical *X* is predominantly a matter of statistics: If *X* (little Johnny who is of average height for a fourteen-year-old) fails to be a typical *X* (say a typical member of his school class of unusually tall boys), then there need not be more than a merely statistical variation—there need not be anything abnormal about him in the sense of a failure to meet the characterizing conditions of an appropriately relevant natural kind.

There are, however, two importantly different sorts of situations with respect to the exception categories. In the one, it is possible to provide a *complete inventory* of the exception cases. A purported illustration of standardistic principles of this first sort is afforded by grammatical and orthographic rules on the order of " 'I' before 'E' except after 'C,' save when sounded as 'A' as in *Neighbor* and *Weigh.*" (The example of "weird" shows that even this rule is standardistic.) In the second, more deep-rooted sort of standardistic situation, the exception categories simply cannot be inventoried completely and comprehensively in advance; no matter how far one goes in this direction, there will always be some further recalcitrant cases that escape one's net. Many standardistic generalizations in the social domain are of this sort, subject to a penumbra of exceptions of potentially indefinite size. Consider the statement, "Normally, people whose marriage survives for twenty years stay together for good." Here various groups of exceptions arise ("couples where one member has a mental breakdown")—indeed so many (or so odd) that we can never categorize them completely in advance. Take the standardistic generalization "Birds can fly." Exceptions include those that never fully developed wings (the kiwi), those that did develop wings that faded into disuse (the ostrich, the dodo), and then there are those with clipped wings, with birth defects, and so on. As a rule, there will, however, be just a few major exception-categories that manage to catch virtually all of the exception cases. (The issue of standardism should itself be approached in a standardistic spirit.)[1]

1. In its ordinary usage, the word "normal" is ambiguious as between a primarily nomic application proceeding against the background of experientially determined "standard conditions of development," and a largely evaluative indication of what people are prepared to acknowledge as acceptable. (In the latter application, the "normal" has a substantially sociopolitical aspect.) This second, more judgmental and evaluative, conception of the "normal" is beside the point of present concerns.

On the basis of these explanations, we can say that "Standardly, *A*s are (are not) *B*s" obtains when:

i. *A*s are generally (very predominantly) *B*s/non-*B*s.
ii. This statistical linkage may, however, have exceptions. But such exceptional cases all (or, perhaps, only *virtually or almost* all) belong to identifiable exception categories, where those exceptions by nature constitute a highly biased sample of the overall population of *A*s.
iii. For each of these exception categories, there is a cogent explanation for why its members fail to conform to the general rule at issue with the generalization in question.[2]

The use of standardized generalizations opens up a variant, literally extraordinary line of reaction to the discovery of exceptions to a generalization. For, on a strictly universalistic approach, there are only two alternatives: (1) to abandon the generalization and search for another, altogether different one; or (2) to dismiss the exception as somehow inapplicable. The shift to standardism opens up yet another alternative: that of *retaining* the generalization (in its standardistic construction) while yet at the same time *accepting* the exception, albeit not by

---

2. A possible refinement of this condition would be to divide the exception categories into the majorly, the middlingly, and the minorly important, and then to rest content when all exceptions of substantial importance can be explained away, without worrying about nonconforming cases in categories at the bottom of the importance scale. But this potentially useful complication will not be pursued here.

dismissing it but by seeing it as an exception—an explicable lapse from the general rule. For as the "cogent explanation" requirement of clause (iii) indicates, standardism requires that the exceptions at issue be cogently explicable as such. This requirement is plausible enough. If it is to make sense to treat some cases as different ("All books circulate to subscribers except reference works and rare books"), then for the generalization to be useful we need a convincing account for why this should be so. There is also the question of why set things up in one way rather than another—for example, in the preceding format, instead of, "No books circulate except for those outside the reference-or-rare category." Just which is the rule and which the exception? These are issues that turn largely on the matter of systematicity and economy of effort: Overall explanatory convenience must be our guide (see Rescher 1989).

Standardism is in its element wherever there are clear-cut exceptions to general rules—where anomalies and deviant cases occur. For when such nonconforming cases exist, we must bend the rules to accommodate them and accordingly confine our generalizations to the normal range. What militates for standardism is the presence of irregularity (ranging from the erratic to the chaotic) that precludes representation through theories formulated in strictly universal laws. In consequence, where there is good reason to think that a given range of phenomena contains singularities or abnormalities, one will be well advised to construe in standardistic terms whatever generalizations are made in the interests of its theoretical systematization.

A useful perspective is afforded by the following contrast among lines of explanatory approach:

- UNIVERSALISM: Addresses issues in terms of entirely synoptic, strictly universal criteria and standards.
- STANDARDISM: Addresses issues in terms of criteria and standards of a restrained generality geared to the normal circumstances of the ordinary course of things.
- PARTICULARISM: Addresses issues in a wholly case-by-case way, forsaking criteria and standards of any generality and proceeding wholly by ad hoc, case-particularized makeshifts.

As this indicates, standardism adopts a metamethodoligical stance intermediate between a rigoristic universalism that sees everything as subject to universal rules and a fragmented particularism that rejects rules altogether and treats everything on a custom-made, case-by-case basis. Its stance is that of a middle-of-the-road position emplaced between two opposed extremes.

Standardized (quasi-universal) generalizations are also closely related to ceteris paribus, "other things being equal" relationships. Consider, for example, "Other things equal, students who study hard get good grades." Precisely because other things ordinarily (normally, as a rule) are equal, this relationship standardly obtains. But it need not always do so—exceptions can and do arise, the exception categories (lesser innate ability, examination anxiety, and the rest) are obvious.

Olaf Helmer and Rescher (1959) stressed long ago the importance in the study of human affairs of those limited, ceteris paribus regularities which do not hold always and everywhere, but only "when other things are equal," as they occasionally are not. (Subsequent writers have deliberated and disputed about the role of such laws in other domains, particularly psychology. See Fodor 1987.) An example of such historical generalizations that are merely "quasi-lawful," is the thesis that "In the France of the *ancien régime*, naval officers were aristocrats," a generalization that reflects a rule admitting occasional but rare exceptions. Clearly all such ceteris paribus regularities—with which the annals of human affairs are replete—call out to be expressed by standardistically interpreted generalizations: They prevail invariably in *normal* cases, but admit of exceptions in extraordinary circumstances. Exactly this sort of thing is at issue with our generalizations when regarded in a standardistic construction. Indeed, in the social domain—the sphere of human affairs—there are few exceptionless laws: The pertinent generalizations virtually always allow exceptions and borderline cases. Like "Birds of a feather flock together," our social generalizations are generally limited to ordinary cases and normal circumstances (which will, of course, differ from one group to another).

2. Standardism and Explanation: The Role of Normalcy

Just how cognitively useful are standardistic generalizations? Above all, can such less than strictly universal linkages bear the weight of *explanatory* employment?

What prevents standardism from being vacuous is the applicability of a distinction between normal and abnormal cases that is *independent* of the particular generalization at issue. Otherwise, clearly the generalization could come down to the trivial, "*X*s are always *Y*s except when they are not." This prospect is blocked on a standardistic approach. For, as stressed earlier, with a standardistic reading of the generalization, exceptions must as a rule belong to certain independently recognizable categories of nonconformity. Unlike statistical generalizations, standardistic uses extend a guarantee of the explicability of exceptions.

Standardism looks to the issue of what happens normally and as a rule. But, of course, the matter of what happens normally (ordinarily, as a rule) is something which, as such, has to be approached from an experiential point of view. This critical aspect of the matter has significant ramifications.

Normality is defined against the background of experience: To be normal is to function as such in the ordinary course of experience. The very idea of *normalcy*—of ordinary rather than extraordinary and anomalous cases, of instances that conform to the customary order of things—is thus a conception that has an indelibly empiricist character. It is clearly geared to the idea of a comparison with "the ordinary course of events" as our experience of the world presents it. The course of experience alone can afford a standard by means of which the contrast between the normal and the abnormal can be implemented: What is normal or not is a matter that hinges crucially and unavoidably on the offerings of our experience. ("Poems have rhyme" looks less plausible when one broadens one's study of literature to include classical antiquity.) The normal is and has to be defined as such by a selectively determined pattern within experience.

Clearly on this basis, standardistic generalities can qualify as yielding perfectly cogent explanations. Consider, for example, the exchange:

Q: Why is *A* the case?

A: Because *B* is the case, and *A* standardly holds in *B*-obtaining situations.

This response clearly provides a perfectly good answer to the initial question. To be sure, the inference:

1. Standardly, *B* obtains whenever *A* does
2. A obtains in this case

———————————

Therefore, *B* obtains

is able to provide an airtight, logically valid argument only at the price of subscribing to the enthymematic premise, "The case at hand is—as far as we can tell—a normal (ordinary, standard) one that fails to belong to various exception categories." And in general, of course, this missing premise poses no problem. In these standardistic situations, explanation is forthcoming under a pervasive presumption of normalcy—and this is something we can generally take for granted, given the established policy of presuming situations to be normal (ordinary, standard) unless and until there are positive indications to the contrary. (On the nature and validation of cognitive policies of this sort see Rescher 1989, chap. 5.) To be sure, someone might now ask for a *reason* why a particular case is seen as a standard one, rather than as belonging to the class of exceptions to the rule. But this concern falls by the wayside once we recognize that in ordinary reasoning as in law a presumption of innocence is operative. Invariably, cases are presumed to belong to the range of the standard and normal until or unless some definite indication suggests otherwise. The "benefit of doubt" is on the side of normalcy. Subject to this standardly prevalent presumption, standardistic generalities do indeed carry explanatory weight. Normalcy is by its very nature an explanatory concept, and, as such, capable of endowing standardistic generalizations with explanatory force in substantiating our answers to questions.

Consider the (essentially true) statement:

(**S**) Spanish does not use "W" (Spanish words do not contain this letter).

Nevertheless, certain words with "W' do indeed occur in Spanish (whisky, windsurfista). The difficulty is resolved through the distinction between ordinary, indigenous Spanish words and "loan words" based on terminology taken from other languages. This distinction manages to salvage the generalization **S** through the modification:

(**S**′) Indigenous Spanish words do not use "W."

To implement *this* premise in the context of subsuming any particular word, we would need to introduce the additional (and usually enthymematic) premise that the word at issue is an ordinary (indigenous) Spanish word. As this example indicates, generalizations are often formulated in ways that tacitly presume that we are dealing with normal (ordinary, standard) cases, thenceforth proceeding on the standing presumption that cases can always be supposed to be ordinary ones in the absence of any specific indications to the contrary. It is this line of thought that prevents the argument:

John is a human being

Therefore, John has one head

from dismissal as a fallacy on grounds of counter-examples. For the argumentation at issue is in fact not fallacious, but simply shorthand for

1. John is a *normal* human being
2. [Normal human beings always have one head]

Therefore, John has one head.

This valid argument salvages its problematic predecessor through the fact that "John is a human being" yields "John is a normal human being" as an immediate inference via the standing presumption that given cases are normal ones absent explicit indications to the contrary. On this basis, a variety of seemingly fallacious arguments just are not. The distinction between *mere* and *normal* cases saves the day. It does so via the second-order distinction between self-sufficient and enthymematic formulations of an argument.

The slack between reality's diversified complexities and standardism's characterization of the *normal* situation parallels the slack between reality's diversified complexities and the natural scientist's characterization of the *ideal* situation (in such contexts as ideal gasses, ideal fluids, and the like). Normality is, in the end, like idealization in its exclusion from preview of certain perfectly actual cases. The recourse to normality means that a sensitivity to context will enter in—a circumstance reflected in the fact that standardism is more useful in the social than in the natural sciences—while the reverse holds for idealization (compare the treatment of idealization in Cartwright 1983 and Nowak 1980). In the "exact" sciences we always refer facts to relationships that are strictly universal, though probabilities may figure internally to their formulation.

A key aspect of standardism is its insistence that exceptions are by and large explicable. Can *these* explanations themselves be standardistic—that is, themselves proceed by means of explanatory generalizations that are construed standardistically?

Consider what this would involve. We start with a generalization of the format:

> *A*s are standardly *B*s—that is, *A*s are always *B*s except in circumstances of type C_1 or C_2 or . . . .

To explain an exception category C_i we need to account for the fact that "While *A*s are generally *B*s, in circumstances C_i, *A*s are non-*B*s." So we need, in effect, to validate a generalization of the form, "In circumstances C_i, *A*s are non-*B*s." But then, of course, this too could transpire via a generalization of the form, "In circumstances C_i, *A*s are normally (ordinarily) non-*B*s." There is thus no reason of principle why standardism cannot be self-instancing, that is, why the explanations it calls for cannot themselves be provided in the standardistic mode.

To be sure, one has to be somewhat careful when throwing together a multitude of standardistic generalizations. We can run into a problem of the sorites type where we have a series along the line of

As are (standardly) *Bs*,
Bs are (standardly) *Cs*,
. . .
Ys are (standardly) *Zs*.

In such cases, even where each and every generalization obtains standardly (ordinarily, as a rule, and so on), it may nevertheless happen that "*As* are (standardly) *Zs*" does not obtain. The piling up of linkages each of which obtains standardistically can, in the end, lead us into a nonstandard situation.

3. Standardism in Philosophy

Philosophy is a purposive enterprise; we pursue it to understand the world we live in and our place within it, seeking answers to our questions in the endeavor to reduce the puzzlement and perplexity that otherwise surrounds us. Yet, its task is not merely to resolve our questions regarding "the big issues" of human concerns and actions in their natural and social context, but to accomplish this in a rationally satisfactory way: What we want from philosophy is not merely answers, but cogent and defensible answers.

Ever since the origination of the classical idea of a "science" in Greek antiquity, most philosophers have geared their aspirations for the discipline to the idea of a science modeled—as was the science of the Greeks—upon *mathematics*. Their goal has been to answer the questions of their field with the precision and universality characteristic of the mathematical sciences. The theories of such a "science," as classically conceived, seek to accomplish their explanatory business in terms of an unqualified universality based on what happens always and everywhere and in all circumstances. The quest for a cognitive grasp of the inherent nomological structure of the world in terms of a deep irrefrangible necessity underlying the world's seemingly fortuitous phenomenal surface has ever been the aspiration of science. The philosophy to which our Greek precursors aspired was to be a science in exactly this sense. (Aristotle's recourse to biologically inspired on-the-whole generalizations was soon shelved in the subsequent tradition.) Accordingly, the quest for philosophical *epistêmê*—for hard and precise mathematicslike knowledge—in philosophical matters characterized the mainstream tradition of philosophy that has come to us from Greek antiquity. In fact, however, this aspiration is deeply problematic.

It is possible—and for various reasons desirable—to contemplate a very different, substantially more modest program for philosophical inquiry that proposes to proceed not in terms of *how on the basis of general principles matters must invariably stand*, but rather in terms of *how as a matter of fact (given the world's realities) matters normally do stand*. Such a less ambitious and empirically oriented philosophy would remain satisfied with securing limited and contingent generalities rather than insisting on unrestricted and exceptionless universality. Foregoing universalistic necessitarianism, it takes a more cautious line and is willing to be guided by the teachings of our experience with the world's course of affairs, and is prepared to carry on its deliberations in the more modest terms of how matters actually do stand in the world's normal course.

Philosophy is now led to take a distinctly "phenomenological" turn in becoming inextricably bound up with the world's realities as the experiential course of things presents them to us. The standardistic approach to philosophical issues which is willing to settle the issues of the field in terms of theses are geared to the usual or normal course of things. The ruling maxim of this mode of philosophizing is, "Project your philosophical views and theories on the basis of a reasonable grasp or the customary course of things—leaving aside concern for bizarre and unusual situations that fly in the face of established patterns and normal circumstances." This variant, *standardistic* mode of philosophizing based on *rules* rather than *scientific laws* opens new and far more promising prospects—though its concern with specifically philosophical issues prevents this enterprise from becoming a natural science proper. (The fact that philosophy may use the scientific facts of life for its explanatory purposes—how else, after all, would a philosophy of nature or a philosophical psychology be possible—does not make philosophy into a natural science.)

Such an approach carries in its wake the prospect of a more modestly conceived philosophy—one prepared to make its claims not with a view of how things must necessarily stand always and universally, but rather with a view oriented at how things generally stand in the normal, ordinary, usual course of things. In its *methodological* stance, philosophical standardism accordingly carries a philosophical empiricism in its wake, seeing that the standard (normal, accustomed) is only determinable as such in a way that does—and must—be reflective of experience.[3] Through its very nature, standardism underwrites an "empirical"

3. Someone might ask, "How can a view of the customary course of matters within the framework of an experience bear on the seemingly nonempirical questions of the philosophy of mathematics or the philosophy of logic?" But this would be naive, for what is involved is not, of course,

conception of the philosophical enterprise as a process of theorizing that is inextricably interconnected with the substance of our (person-variable) experience with the issues that occupy our attention.

The theorist who has perhaps most emphatically stressed the standardistic aspect of philosophical conceptions is R. G. Collingwood. He characterized the pivotal phenomenon as "the overlap of classes." For him, philosophical generalizations of a rigidly universal sort—be it affirmative like "All *A*s are *B*s" (which excludes the *A*s from the non-*B*s) or negative like "No *A*s are *B*s" (which excludes the *A*s from the *B*s)—are always inappropriate because whenever the *A*s and *B*s represent philosophically germane classes or categories, there will never be sharp boundaries that avert the prospect of deviant "borderline" cases, "The specific classes of a philosophical genus do not exclude one another, but overlap. This overlap is not exceptional, it is normal; and it is not negligible in extent, it may reach formidable proportions" (Collingwood 1933, 3).[4] As Collingwood stressed, "imperfect" generalizations of the sort

---

our *sensory* experience of interaction with the physical world, but our *conceptualizing* experience with the issues of the domain—including abstracts like arguments, structures, numbers, and so on.

4. To all appearances, Collingwood's bold generalization is problematic on its own grounds, for "All philosophical generalizations are problematic" carries obvious consequences for this generalization itself. Here,

that standardism typifies are bound to play a key role in philosophical theorizing.

Economics, John Hicks insisted, is a discipline, not a science, because its "laws" are never rigid. They always depend on a ceteris paribus clause, and their applicability hinges "on the correctness of the supposition that the variables of which they have taken account are the only ones that matter" (Hicks 1983, 371). The present view of the philosophical situation is rather analogous. It sees philosophical generalizations as depending not on ceteris paribus assumptions but rather on assumptions of normalcy. And it sees the applicability of philosophy's generalization as hinging on the correctness of the supposition that the factors being taken into account function in the case at hand in the ordinary, normal way. On this perspective, philosophy too can be characterized as a discipline rather than a science. Instead of being yet another entry on the register of sciences, it represents the attempt to articulate and to explicate the standards already inherent in all of our intellectual and practical enterprises in their relation to the traditional "big issues" regarding ourselves and our place in the world's scheme of things.

---

as with many philosophical doctrines (e.g., skepticism), the table-turning argument (*peritropê*) deployed by Socrates against the Protagoras of Plato's *Theaetetus* is once again serviceable. Such issues of reflexivity will be pursued in chapter 7.

Philosophical standardism opts for modesty in a complex world. It calls for abandoning pretentions to universality and inevitability, instead shifting our attention to normal circumstances and ordinary cases. Gearing its philosophizing not to the necessities of abstract general principles, but to the actualities that our cognitive commerce with the world reveals to us, philosophical standardism abandons the traditional a priori stance of mainstream Western philosophy in favor of one that is a posteriori and experientially oriented. It does not try to resolve issues in terms of how things must necessarily go as a matter of theoretical general principle, but rather proceeds in terms of how things do normally go as best we can determine the matter. Rather than looking to general principles of abstract necessity, it proceeds in an empirical spirit; it looks for guidance to *experience*—with all its characteristic contingencies and potential incompleteness.

Viewing the issues in this light indicates that postmodern critiques have it wrong. The flaw of classical philosophy is not so much an exaggerated commitment to *certainty* as one to a *precision* that is simply unavailable in philosophy's problem context, given the nature of the information we have to work with via the data at our disposal.

The present book will examine and defend such a standardistic approach to philosophy—an approach that abandons inflatedly universalistic and necessitarian pretentions for this field and adopts a less ambitious, more descriptive and "empirical" line. But why should we rest content with this more modest and "realistic" mode of philosophizing? What sorts of rationale underwrites its appropriateness? Such questions define the focal issue of this book.

TWO

The Standardistic Approach to Philosophical Issues

SYNOPSIS

(1) Standardism has an important role to play in philosophy. The workaday concepts we use in everyday life—and in much of philosophy as well—are fact-coordinated in being geared to our experience-based view about how things work in the real world. Their link to the world's perceived facts ties these concepts to the conditions that characterize the normal course of things as our experience presents it. (2) It accordingly makes good sense to adopt an experientially geared standardistic approach in philosophy because the basic concepts of our philosophical deliberations are rooted in the communicative setting of ordinary life and must therefore reflect our experience-based understanding of the world's course of things. (3) Increased security can generally be obtained for one's claims at the price of decreased precision. Science favors precision over security, while our ordinary-life discourse takes the reverse line. Here, standardistically oriented philosophy sides with ordinary life: It too favors security over precision, and it takes its stand on how things generally go in the world. (4) The nature of philosophical issues is such that if we adopt an idealized version of science as our model and will only be satisfied with establishing theses that are strictly universal and necessary, then we will come up

empty-handed. Standardism with its empirical approach affords our best promise for obtaining answers to our philosophical questions that are at once informative and defensible. (5) In view of the very nature of its mission, philosophy cannot simply abandon those "imprecise" concepts of our presystematic discourse.

1. Fact-Laden Concepts

Philosophical standardism is based on two leading ideas: (1) that tenable generalizations in philosophy are in general not rigid but flexible (porous, permeable, fuzzy, or the like) in that they admit of exceptions; (2) that where this occurs—when exceptions are realized—this fact is explicable, that is, there is an explanatory rationale for categorizing those anomalous cases as actual exceptions, so that the normative force of these generalizations survives substantially intact despite those violations. But what is it about the inherent problem situation of philosophy that grounds the appropriateness of taking this standardistic view of its generalizations?

The problems of philosophy—those big questions about life, the world, and the human condition—are rooted in questions that we pose in the language of our everyday experience and discourse. If they are to be answered satisfactorily, they must, in the end, be answered in these ordinary terms. But ordinary language—is designed for practical purposes. It is a medium for the transmission of opinion and sentiment about the workaday world of our everyday experience. It thus embodies the assumptions and presuppositions built into our commonplace view of things reflective of the common course of our experience.

The development of ordinary language and its transmission across generations root in the necessity and desirability of our communicating with one another about the world we live in. The conceptions we generally employ in everyday life inhere in a language that is designed with a view to its application to reality. Their very reason for being is to enable us to categorize, describe, and explain what goes on in the world about us. They are predicated on beliefs and assumptions geared to the actual as we experience and interpret it, enabling us to orient ourselves cognitively in our world. If this concept machinery were not fitted to our experience of the world about us, it would be much useless baggage which, for that very reason, would have been abandoned long ago even if, *per impossibile,* it had evolved in the first place. The linguistic mechanisms of ordinary discourse thus have to reflect the general course of our shared experiences because they would not exist as such if they did not do so. The gearing of our language to our experience is a precondition of its very being.

The familiar and prominent concepts we find enshrined in the language are literally *mundane* in that they reflect our beliefs as to how matters stand

and how things work in the world. In particular, they are bound to reflect the normal, ordinary course of things in which various theoretically separable factors actually go together. It is a truism that life consists primarily of the ordinary and commonplace. The obvious corollary is that the conceptual instruments we devise for the communicative handling of our experiences become geared to the ordinary, commonplace, and normal.

This state of affairs endows our philosophically germane concepts with a certain imprecision that always leaves room for conflict and incompatibility. In consequence of this, the conception of nonrigidly standardistic generalizations provides a powerful tool for philosophical problem solving. For philosophy arises not so much from awe and wonder as from perplexity and puzzlement. Many, if not most, philosophical problems root in aporetic situations where we face a hard choice among individually plausible but collectively inconsistent contentions. (The reasons for this situation and the modalities of its management are examined in detail in Rescher 1985.) Consider, for example, the following aporetic cluster of individually plausible but collectively incompatible theses:

- Promise breaking is morally wrong: Promise breakings are always moral transgressions.
- It is never morally wrong to do what we cannot possibly help doing: Doing something one cannot help is never a case of moral transgression.

- In some circumstances one cannot help breaking a promise (for example, when circumstances beyond one's control preclude one from honoring it).

Clearly, on purely logical grounds these three plausible-seeming theses are collectively incompatible: one or another of them must be rejected. Considering that the third thesis is simply a fact of life, it results that, to all appearances, considerations of mere logical consistency constrain us to abandon one of those two initial contentions. But if one is willing to give those initial two generalizations a standardistic (rather than rigidly universal) reading, the incompatibility at issue at once vanishes. By softening these generalizations we preserve their tenability. Here, as often, the edge of a philosophical conflict can be blunted by a standardistic construction of our generalizations, enabling us to retain what we wish to maintain substantially intact in the face of collective inconsistencies. And there is good reason of general principles why philosophical generalizations should be softened in this sort of way.

Attuned in the first instance to the requirements of practical purpose and the needs of efficient communication in real-life conditions, our philosophical concepts are geared to factual presuppositions—and, above all, to factual assumptions as to how things normally and ordinarily run in the world. Not that philosophy as such is a standardly empirical inquiry. Its deliberations are basically conceptual and the empirical aspect comes in through the back door, as it were. The salient point is that the concepts it deploys function in such a way as to incorporate a view of the empirical facts. One cannot satisfactorily elaborate their conceptual relationships without taking account of the experiential realities on which they are predicated. With the fact-oriented concepts of philosophical relevancy, semantical and factual considerations become intertwined: Pure analysis can at best sort them out; it can bring to light the factual aspect of the concept, but it can in no way mitigate or remove this empirical aspect of reference to a factual background of experience. Where our concepts have factual presuppositions, any prospect of a neat dichotomy of "empirical" versus "conceptual" goes by the board. At such points, the two issues become fused into a seamless whole. And philosophizing itself then becomes a (partially) empirical enterprise, notwithstanding its involvements with "conceptology." (Some of the considerations of this section are dealt with in greater detail in Rescher 1993.)

2. Philosophy Is Geared to the Conceptional Perspective of the Ordinary Course of Life

In the course of their explanatory efforts philosophers invoke generalizations. They deploy theses like:

- All factual knowledge originates in the senses: *nihil est in intellectu quod non prius fuerit in sensu.*
- All duties are rooted in rules: Whenever *X* has an obligation to do *A*, this is so in virtue of an appropriate general rule *R* stipulating that in *X*'s circumstances *A* is the obligatory thing to do.
- All existence is substance-connected: Whatever exists is either a substance (a *thing* of some sort) or else a property or feature of things.

Generalizations of this sort constitute the heart and core of philosophical doctrines as we generally have them. But need they—nay, *should* they—be taken as strictly universal contentions? Or might it make better sense to construe them as stating not how things *must always* be rather than as maintaining how things *do normally* stand?

The motivating rationale for such a change of approach to philosophical generalizations lies deep in the nature of the concerns of this discipline. The complex spiders' webs spun in philosophical theorizing are always attached to "the real world" of everyday life and its scientific refinements. Even a superficial look at the various subdivisions or branches of philosophy shows that they are virtually always rooted in matters of prephilosophical, everyday-life concern. The materials of "human experience," in all the manifold senses of this conception, constitute the *raison d' être* of our philosophizing. The reflexive, second-order discipline of metaphilosophy aside, the issues of philosophy revolve about extraphilosophical matters. Preeminently, philosophical questions arise in terms of the concepts of common life. The central concepts of philosophy ("mind," "matter," "causality," "nature," "reality," "truth," "knowledge," "agency," "personhood," "good," "right," "justice," and such) are importations from the thought world of everyday life where they serve in the cognitive manipulation of everyday experience. When philosophers deal with *truth*, or *beauty*, or *goodness*, or *justice*, they are concerned with these ideas as they function in our everyday discussions and deliberations; they are certainly *not* proposing to address technical conceptions that are disjoint or distinct from the ways in which we ordinarily deliberate and talk about the issues. They may be seeking a "rational reconstruction" of everyday usage in the manner of Carnap (see Carnap 1962, sec. 2). But here too the nature of the usage one is attempting to reconstruct remains the focal point. Philosophy—after all—addresses problems that arise out of our attempts to make sense of the world as our experience presents it.

Now, the basic concepts in whose terms we transact our experiential business are in general infused with our understanding of the world's facts. These concepts are not designed for use in "every possible world," but for use in *this* world. They arise from the need to handle communicatively the materials of our experience, and are geared to the realities that we encounter and manipulate in the course of everyday life. Their import and their applicability relate to how matters *do* stand, and not to how they *might* conceivably stand by some "stretch of the imagination." They are concerned with our understanding of the world's actual arrangements and their component elements are connected by contingent rather than necessary linkages. Even when philosophers deliberate normatively about how things *should* be (in contrast to how they actually are), they are nevertheless concerned primarily with some aspect of the real (with how you or I should behave, and not how the nonexistent individuals of some nonexistent world should comport themselves). In consequence, philosophical deliberations rest on a basis of reality-geared fact or supposition, connected to the world as our experience indicates it to be.[1]

The concepts we standardly use to think about the arrangements of the real—and which accordingly lie at the basis of our philosophical reflec-

1. This is least clear with respect to those philosophical theories that address issues of "pure" mathematics and logic—those at work in metamathematics and metalogic, and those appertaining to regions very far removed from our everyday experience of the *physical* world. But they are not, of course, comparably removed from the realm of our conceptualizing experience. The objects of mathematics (numbers and structures) may have no "natural history," but this is clearly *not* the case with respect to our conceptualizing *thought* about such objects.

tions—are of an essentially *composite* character. But rather than representing a combination of elements united by purely theoretical considerations, *the concurrence involved in such concepts rests on a strictly empirical or experiential foundation.* Their unity is a unity of experience, as the following illustrations show:

- Our concept of PERSONAL IDENTITY views the sameness of persons through a fusion of *bodily continuity* (tracking through space and time) and *continuity of personality* (memory, habits, tastes, dispositions, skills,) (Moreover, each of these is itself composite.)
- Our concept of PERSONS involves the conjoining of *mind* and *body*, and preserves a mutually accordant functioning of mental and bodily activity, thus manifesting two very different sets of characteristic powers and dispositions.
- Our concept of VALUE (in the sense of "social justice is something he values") fuses three sorts of factors: covert ("mentalistic" thought, motivation, rationalization), transitional (verbal behavior in affording *vis-à-vis* others some defense, explanation, or justification of one's acts), and overt (actual physical behavior).
- Our concept of BELIEF coordinates mentalistic dispositions to think and overt physicalistic dispositions to action.

Let us consider the last example in some detail. Observe that both key factors at issue in belief mental disposition and overt behavior in appropriate circumstances must come together before we speak of believing. His mental condition alone does not establish that actually *X* believes that a bomb is to explode shortly in the room if his every act belies this (under suitable conditions—e.g., he has no wish to commit suicide). But evasive behavior alone will not clinch the matter either if sufficient evidence of *X*'s every thought—tacit and professed—indicates that he is nowise under an impression that a bomb is present. Both sets of factors—mind states and action dispositions—must be suitably coordinated before we can unproblematically speak of *X*'s having a belief. Otherwise, we could not appropriately say simply that *X* believes that *P*, but would have to use some such complex circumlocution as "*X*, while not accepting *P* is the case, acts as though it were," "*X*, while maintaining that *P* is the case certainly does not behave (say, by betting) in an accordant fashion," or the like. These cognitive and behavioral dispositions both come together in the composite idea of a belief. Their consilience and consonance is not a matter of abstract principle, however, but rather one of fact—of how experience indicates that things usually go in the world.

And this case is typical. For the fact is that all of those various philosophically critical concepts are both multicriterial and fact-coordinative:

- They are *multicriterial* because in each case a plurality of (in principle separable) components is involved; for example, in the case of personal identity, both bodily continuity and continuity of personality play a pivotal role. (The discussion of cluster concepts in Wittgenstein 1953 bears upon this issue.)

- They are *fact-coordinative* because in each case the theoretically separable but concept-joined criterial factors are held together in an integrative fusion by facts or purported facts, that is, by our view of how the world actually works. (Thus in the case of personal identity we find that bodily continuity and continuity of personality generally and standardly go together.)

Concepts of this fact-coordinative sort conjoin factors whose unity is a matter of experience. They rest on presuppositions whose content is factual, reflecting a view of how things go in the world. They are empirically conditioned, being developed and deployed against an experiential backdrop—a *Weltanschauung*, or rather some miniscule sector thereof. The crucial contribution of such an empirical basis is to underwrite the de facto conjoining of a plurality of factors that are in principle separable from one another. Because these factors are thus coordinated, we are *spared any need to make up our mind* as to which of them is ultimately determinative or decisive for the concept's applicability. Experience assures that certain purely theoretical possibilities are of no effective practical concern because the things they split apart actually go together.

The concepts in whose terms philosophical theses and theories are articulated are accordingly fact-laden through their gearing to "the domain of experience," that is, to the way in which things usually and normally go. Such conceptual machinery hinges on "the ordinary course of things" as we actually encounter it. It reflects our experience of the world by indicating how things standardly go in the domain of what comes to our notice. This feature of its conceptual frame of reference must inevitably inform and condition the way in which we can transact our philosophical business. It means that we must—or should—recognize philosophy's commitment to "the real world," albeit in a way very different from the commitment of orthodox science—and of traditional philosophy.

3. The Cognitive Stance of Science versus That of Ordinary Life

Throughout the sphere of our cognitive concerns there is an inherent tension between generality and security. Increased security can generally be purchased for our claims at the price of decreased accuracy and precision. We estimate the height of a tree at around 25 feet. We are *quite sure* that the tree is 25 ± 3 feet high. We are *virtually certain* that its height is 25 ± 10 feet. But we are *completely and absolutely sure,* when the item at issue is indeed a tree, that its height is between 1 inch and 100 yards.

Of this we are "totally sure" and "certain beyond the shadow of a doubt," "as certain as we can be of anything in the world," "so sure that we would be willing to stake our life on it," and the like. For any sort of plausible claim whatsoever, there is always a characteristic trade-off between its evidential *security* (or probability), on the one hand, and, on the other, its contentual *definiteness* (exactness, detail, precision, and such). The prevailing situation is as depicted by the concave curve presented in figure 2.1. Throughout the range of our information-gathering inquiries, the epistemic lay of the land is

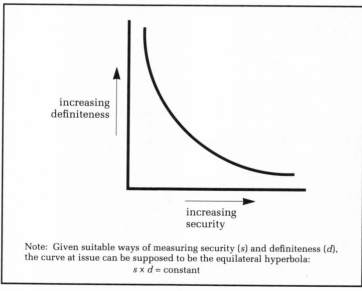

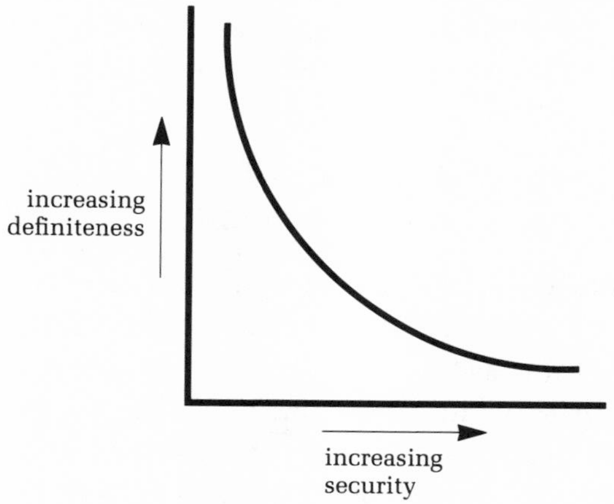

Note: Given suitable ways of measuring security (s) and definiteness (d), the curve at issue can be supposed to be the equilateral hyperbola:

$$s \times d = \text{constant}$$

FIGURE 2.1 *The Decline of Security with Increasing Definiteness*

such that it is impracticable to make one's generalization at once both highly interesting (i.e., general) and highly safe (i.e., secure). In philosophy, above all, the price we have to pay for achieving tenable theories is to curtail their sweep.

Traditionally, science seeks to operate at the top of the diagram. It forgoes the security of indefiniteness in striving for the maximal achievable universality, precision, exactness, and the like. The mathematically precise law claims of natural science involve no hedging, no fuzziness, no incompleteness, and no exceptions; they are *strict:* precise, wholly explicit, exceptionless. When investigating the melting point of lead, physicists have no interest in claiming that *most* pieces of (pure) lead will *quite likely* melt at *somewhere around* this temperature. (Even when science deals in probabilities, it deals with them in a way that characterizes *exactly* how they must comport themselves.)

By contrast, the ground rules of ordinary-life discourse are altogether different. Here we operate at the right-hand side of the diagram. When *we* assert in ordinary life that "peaches are delicious," we mean something like "most people will find the eating of suitably grown and duly matured peaches are relatively pleasurable experience." Such statements have all sorts of built-in hedges and safeguards like "more or less," "in ordinary circumstances," "by and large," "normally," "if other things are equal," and the like. They are not laws in the usual sense, but rules of thumb; that is, a matter of practical lore rather than scientific rigor. In natural science, we deliberately accept risk by aiming at maximal definiteness and thus at maximal informativeness and testability; but in ordinary life, matters stand differently. After all, ordinary-life communication is a practically oriented endeavor carried on in a social context: It stresses such maxims as "Aim for security, even at the price of definiteness;" "Protect your credibility;" "Avoid misleading people, or—even worse—lying to them by asserting outright falsehoods;" "Do not take a risk and 'cry wolf'." The aims of ordinary-life discourse are primarily geared to the processes of social interaction and the coordination of human effort. In this context, it is crucial that we seek to maintain credibility and acceptance in our communicative efforts, that is, that we establish and maintain a good reputation for reliability and trustworthiness. In the framework of common-life discourse, we thus take our stance at a point far removed from that of a mathematically precise "science" as this domain was traditionally cultivated. Our concern is perforce not with the precise necessities but with the looser commonalities of things.

The crucial fact for present purposes is that in this matter of definiteness versus security, as in others, philosophy stands on the side of everyday life. The issues are so large and complex and the data we have are so tenuous in their bearing, that we have little realistic choice but to compromise definiteness (generality, precision, universality) for the sake of security (tenability, plausibility). If we are not content to join the skeptic in leaving the arena of deliberation empty-handed, then we have to be realistic about what the deliberations of philosophy can actually accomplish. Forgoing all unrealistic demands for an unrealizable perfection in our philosophizing, we have to make the most we can of the possibilities that are, in a realistic sense of the term, actually *available* to us. Rather than hankering after abstract connections that hold exceptionlessly for any imaginable world, we are to look to what is standardly (normally) true in the actual world we live in.

Aristotle's biology and physics was full of general rules to which there are sporadic exceptions. The rules say how things go "on the whole" (*hôs epi to polu:* in general); the exceptions "prove" the rule. But this points toward a premodern conception of science that the necessitarianism of early modern (i.e., prestatistical) science simply abandoned. In science we may indeed be able to get by with the dichotomy of *either strictly universal or merely statistical*. But in philosophy we cannot. For better or worse, the spirit of Aristotelian science is still with us here and we cannot dispense with sub-universal but nevertheless normatively laden generalizations.

Standardism provides our best practicable route to security in philosophical generalization. Humans are innovative beings, capable of a deliberate introduction of novelty. Through intellectual insight and practical ingenuity, intelligent agents are able to bring into being things that have not previously been in existence, and, in particular, to achieve new knowledge about old issues. Such innovation—be it in intellectual or physical matters—is by its very nature a venture in pattern breaking. It alters the landscape of what has heretofore been the case. But while innovation and the broadening of horizons generally alters what *has always been* the case, it is less likely to change what is *normally* the case. Clearly, the fabric of standardistic (rather than universalistic) generalizations is far less susceptible to being disturbed by novelty.

In philosophy, our most promising pathway to reasonable security lies by way of curtailing the "scientific" pretentions of our claims. When we generalize in the manner of saying that people pursue life, liberty, and happiness we do not achieve rigid universality but operate on a standardistic plane. What standardism would accordingly have us do is to forgo—or at least radically curtail—our aspirations to necessitarianism in philosophy. (A standardism true to its own spirit cannot, of course, insist on the rigid impossibility of ever securing necessary truths.)

4. The Danger of Asking Too Much

Its insistence on avoiding dogmatism by refusing to lay down rules beyond the prospect of exception—this very rule itself included—is what characterizes standardism and sets it apart from the fixation of traditional philosophy on what is rigidly necessary and strictly universal. The salient feature of standardism is its relaxed approach to generalizations, that is, its willingness to contemplate what is normally so, instead of hankering after what must be so invariably and exceptionlessly. It is content to let us talk about how matters stand "in the first approximation" rather than strictly and solely "in the final analysis." Standardism is prepared to pursue the process of generalization in a manner that is more "realistic" and "relaxed" than anything that traditional philosophy is prepared to contemplate.

But just why should we draw in our philosophical horns in such a manner? Why should one abandon the science-imitating universalistic/necessitarian line of traditional philosophizing in favor of the generalistic/normalistic formulations of a more relaxed, humanistic approach? Primarily because we ought to be realistic. For their rooting in the inherently normalistic concepts of everyday discussion requires philosophical issues to be addressed in standardistic terms. Philosophy, after all, takes its departure from a concern for our workaday human affairs: Even its concern for "the world" is (unlike that of natural science) anthropocentrically us-oriented, ultimately preoccupied with the bearing of the issues on *our* concerns—on our knowledge, our role, our prospects, and so on. Preeminently, philosophy's concern with logic is as an instrumentality of *our* reasoning, and with cosmology as an explanation of *our* universe. This focus upon the human dimension has important ramifications, for universal generalizations in human affairs are almost invariably undermined by their essentially chaotic aspect, that is, by the ineliminable role of chance and luck in matters of human concern. The general rules that can be laid down to characterize our situation—be it in ethics, in epistemology, in metaphysics, or wherever—have to be geared to the general course of things because unusual and unforeseeable confluences and complications can almost always intrude to upset the applecart. With the human concerns at stake in philosophy, chaos, so to speak, can and often does intervene to call off all the usual bets, abrogating the usual order of things to which our generalizations are—and must be—attuned.

The obvious difficulty of universalistic and necessitarian philosophizing is its commitment to uniformity and universality—to the idea that the relevant relationships can generally be captured in one unrestrictedly exceptionless rule. This contemplates a conceptual tidiness that may indeed be present in pure mathematics, but is very questionable in matters of philosophy. For the issues we deal with in philosophy are inextricably rooted in the concepts of everyday life. The factors at issue are not technical artifacts projected for their abstract interest, but must always be representable in terms of the commonplace descriptive machinery of our everyday communication. Accordingly, they simply do not admit of a purely theoretical systematization that abstracts from the experienced course of things.

In philosophical matters, our prospects of establishing rigorously universal theses are unpromising. Reluctant to face this fact, however, philosophers have generally striven to answer their questions in terms of claims regarded as universal, necessary, and a priori. Traditionally they look to the *exact* sciences—logic and mathematics—as their model. But as the history of the subject shows all too clearly, these programmatic ambitions have produced great problems. By asking too much, philosophers have in consequence obtained too little. Their demands for a *conjoint* realization of high definiteness and high security has put them "off the curve" of epistemic feasibility, so that they are in the end destined to failure. A not insignificant part of the reason for philosophical controversy and dissensus lies in the effective impossibility of securing an adequate probative/evidential basis for the sort of exaggeratedly ambitious claims that are traditionally projected in this domain. The nature of philosophical issues is such as to pose the ever-present threat that if we will only be satisfied with theses that are absolutely universal and necessary, we will wind up with having nothing at all.

A standardistic focus upon the usual (rather than necessary) course of things accordingly becomes a sensible and realistic proposition. For standardism enables us to achieve various important desiderata:

- an increased security for our theses;
- an improved methodological grasp—it being far easier to spot how things generally go than to establish that they must always and invariably stand in a certain wise; and
- an enhanced persuasiveness for our position—it being much simpler to convince people that things standardly and normally X-wise than to convince them that they must be so inevitably.

It is, in sum, not insignificantly to the advantage of standardism in philosophy that with respect to the large issues of the field normality is incomparably easier to secure than rigid universality, seeing that an appeal to commonalities of people's experience, to their sense of the ordinary and primitive course of things, is something both straightforward and convincing.

The overly ambitious nature of classically necessitarian philosophy makes it effectively impossible to provide resolutions to the problems that cogently convince people of their acceptability. An empirical approach, by contrast, offers promise of greater effectiveness in the realization of more limited objectives. It offers the prospect of achieving a plausible resolution of issues that we would otherwise simply be unable to resolve in an even halfway satisfactory way. Accordingly, an empirical approach that is satisfied with theses geared to how things stand generally and usually (rather than universally and necessarily) affords our best promise for retaining answers to our philosophical questions in a way that is at once informative, defensible, and adequate to the problem situation of the philosophical domain.

By asking for more, that is, by insisting on principles that are absolutely universal and necessary, we would effectively assure ourselves of getting nothing at all. The problems are so intricate, the issues so complex, the evidence so tenuous, that by demanding theses of a high degree of precision and definiteness we render it impossible to evidentiate *anything* with a degree of security adequate to the realization of intellectual comfort. In philosophical contexts, we can (generally) do not better than to support theses regarding how matters stand *in general* with respect to the questions at issue; in this domain, strict generalizations are (generally) not cogently substantiable. Insofar as we want viable answers—insofar as the security and tenability is a goal of ours—we are well advised to proceed conservatively, staking our philosophical claims in a way that is cautious and qualified. And so, standardism comes into its own.

Historically, philosophers have all too often seen philosophizing as a labor of pure reason, holding with Spinoza that it "is not in the nature of reason to regard things not as contingent, but as necessary" (*Ethics*, II, 44). They construe philosophizing as committed to necessitarian aspirations by its very nature as a venture in rational inquiry. But the ample course of our experience with the discipline indicates that this position is altogether unavailing—that in philosophy, as elsewhere, reason without experience is blind. And once we accept this, and acknowledge that philosophizing too has an experiential dimension by virtue of which its deliverances become to some extent contingent and vulnerable to the cold winds of experiential change, then we must also acknowledge that the deliverances of philosophy will not stand secure against novelty of circumstance, but will be fragile and defeasible in the light of the altered conditions unfolding in a world where chance and chaos play a significant role. A philosophical doctrine must be flexible; it cannot stand fixed and unchanging but must, like all else that has life, learn to adapt—or else die.

Consider just one example. Historically, logical positivism came to grief because its champions could no longer defend the distinctions pivotal to its articulation (analytic/synthetic, conceptual/factual, and so on) against the challenges and objections that could be—and were— made against such procrustean dichotomies. Both the supporters and opponents of positivism saw such distinctions as being absolutely hard and fast—universal and absolute. The idea of a standardistic softening of these dichotomies—of linking their applicability to normal issues and ordinary circumstances—did not occur to these disputants. But once this prospect arises, matters look very different. Take the analytic/synthetic distinction between what is true on conventional and what is true on factual grounds. To investigate the tenability of "All (unbroken) knives have blades," it would be foolish indeed to inspect the knives in our kitchen drawers or our museums. Linguistic usage suffices: if an implement does not have a blade we just do not *call* it a knife. Statements like "Knives have blades" are thus clearly analytic. On the other hand, "No Minoan knives were made of steel" cannot be investigated on the basis of linguistic usage alone; we have to go out into "the real world" and examine artifacts. Such statements are clearly synthetic. The distinction involved is clear enough for the standard situation of normal cases where it is possible to understand and implement the issues in a more or less straightforward way. The analytic/synthetic distinction runs into trouble only if we seek to operate by means of universal rules that are to apply rigidly all across the board in an altogether hard-

and-fast way. Had the positivists approached their concerns in the more relaxed manner of a standardistic approach, their doctrine would have taken on a more flexible and vastly more tenable guise (albeit in a way that conflicts direly with their pretentious to mathematico-scientific precision).

It could, of course, be objected that this diminution of demands is incompatible with the very nature of philosophy. For whether one likes it or not, many or most philosophers have in fact been committed to the pursuit of strictly universal necessity. But of course, it is one thing to ask for something and another to obtain it. The merit of standardism's lowering of demands lies exactly in the fact that this affords a better prospect of achieving meaningful answers to our philosophical questions and providing for viable resolutions of the problems of the field.

Its seeming weakness is actually the basis of philosophical standardism's strength. For given the complexity of the issues, such an "empirical"—that is, experience-geared—approach that rests satisfied with theses geared to how things stand generally and usually (rather than universally and necessarily) affords our best prospect for obtaining answers to our philosophical questions in a way that is at once informative and defensible. When we address those "big issues" of human nature and action in their natural and social context, our chances of securing viable answers are vastly improved by looking to the usual course of things rather than pursuing the will-o'-the-wisp of abstract general principles in a quest for strictly exceptionless universality. The aspirations of a standardistic philosophy may be more modest, but they are for that very reason also much more realistic. If we indeed *want* answers to our philosophical problems we have to be prepared to accept them as they are in practice attainable.

5. Why Philosophy Cannot Simply Abandon Those "Imprecise" Concepts of Presystemic Discourse

Given that the ordinary concepts in whose terms we communicate about our everyday experiences cannot serve traditional philosophy's idealized demands, why not simply abandon them altogether in this domain? For good reason. To do so would have the serious drawback of effectively leaving the traditional arena of philosophical discussion. Those "imperfect and imprecise" concepts provide the raw materials for philosophy and are an essential part of its concerns. The issues with which our philosophizing begins, and for the sake of whose understanding and elucidation it carries on its work, are taken in the first instance from the realm of experience. Those presystematic concepts characterize the ways in which we conceive of the experience which is the stuff of life, and thus ultimately the stuff of philosophy as well.

The concepts that figure centrally in philosophical discussions are always borrowed from everyday life or from its elaboration in science. The discussions of philosophy always maintain some connection to these pre- or extraphilosophical notions; they cannot simply rid themselves of those standard conceptions that are the flesh and blood of our thinking in everyday life. The philosophers' "knowledge" and "ignorance," their "right" and their "wrong" must be those of ordinary people, or at least keep very close to them. The philosophers' "space" and "time" and "matter" must be those of the natural scientist. In abandoning the concepts of our prephilosophical concerns in favor of word creations of some sort, the philosopher thereby also abandons the problems that constitute the enterprise's very reason for being. To talk *wholly* in terms of technical concepts that differ from the ordinary ones as radically as the physicist's concept of *work* differs from the layperson's notion is in effect to change the subject. Whatever appeal this step may have, it is not one that we can take *within* the framework of the professed objective of a clarificatory analysis of philosophical issues. It is neither candid nor helpful to pass off the wolf of concept abandonment as the sheep of concept clarification. It would be a deeply mistaken procedure to practice conceptual "clarification" in such a manner as to destroy the very items we are purportedly clarifying.

Of course, philosophers are free to invent their own language and to introduce their own technical terminology. But if they are to use it for communicating with nonphilosophers, they must explain it, and this is something they have to do in a language that others can understand: the language of everyday life. Their gearing to the normal, ordinary course of things means that the concepts of everyday life—and those of philosophy with them—resist the introduction of surgical precision. They lack that merely abstract integrity of purely conceptual coherence that alone could enable them to survive in the harsh light of theoretical clarity.

The issues that constitute philosophy's prime mission are not, at bottom, technical matters domestic to the field itself. They are issues that arise in the conditions of everyday life and in the sciences; they are questions not, to be sure, *within* but rather *about* these domains of experience. Without them, philosophy would lose its point, its very reason for being. The technical issues of philosophy are always a means toward prephilosophical ends. We address philosophical issues to resolve further issues that enable us to resolve yet further issues, and so on, until at last we arrive back at questions posed in the prephilosophical lingua franca of human experience. Its connectability to those presystemic issues of our experiential world that are the very reason for being of our philosophical concerns is an inherent aspect of what makes philosophy the enterprise at is.

All mind-directed activity, theoretical and practical alike, proceeds with reference to implicit pretheoretical standards (cognitive, practical, moral, and so on). But often as not their implementation is not up to the demands of theoretical precision. However, the task of philosophical elucidation is not to abolish these imperfections but to clarify them and to harmonize them in the best realizable way. Such clarifications enable us to become self-comprehending: We now know better what before we saw only through a glass, darkly. Philosophy clarifies, energizes, and to some extent rationalizes and reforms our presystematic ideas, beliefs, and commitments, but it does not—cannot—abrogate them. (Nor can it provide them with an external, altogether "presupposition-free" basis or foundation for their justification.)[2]

Philosophers cannot at one and the same time practice their craft and forsake the everyday and

2. Not only have all attempts at providing such "absolute" foundations failed, but they are in fact predestined to fail. Any attempt to articulate such a validating theory can make sense only in the setting of a preestablished standard of adequacy and thus widen the framework of those very pretheoretical standards that we are allegedly trying to validate. We can neither validate those pretheoretical standards in a wholly theoretical manner nor yet dispense with them, and recognizing this status of affairs is a part of what philosophical wisdom is all about.

scientific conceptions that provide the stage setting of their discipline. Philosophers are thus caught between a rock and a hard place—unable to accept those experientially biased conceptions of prephilosophical usage wholly at face value, and yet unable to live without them because the core problems of the field take their root and draw their life from them. (On these issues see the Introduction to Rorty 1967.)

If the deliberations of philosophy were not interconnected with those of human experience through a process of conceptual interlinkage, then they would thereby become *pointless*. Philosophers' claim to address the problems that arise and are initially posed in our prephilosophical conceptions would ring hollow if the results achieved had no discernible relationship to them. To cease to ask about the role of value of the world, about humanity's place in its scheme of things, and about our interrelations with our fellows is to give up the very project at issue. To abandon those big questions that arise in the context of our empirical interaction with the world is to abandon philosophy itself. The very reason for being of the philosophical enterprise lies in its historic mission to resolve our questions about the world as they actually arise for us in terms of the concepts and categories of everyday life. To abandon this enterprise is to "change the subject", and while positivistically minded philosophers have, in all times and places, advocated just this, this course is at odds with the palpable interest and importance of the issues.

Technical philosophy accordingly no more *abolishes* that ultimate level of prephilosophically experiential issues than scientific medicine *abolishes* those prescientific symptoms and disabilities toward whose management its efforts are ultimately directed. Philosophers need to have recourse to the terminology of experience in everyday life and in science which provides the ultimate terms of reference for philosophical deliberations. Maintaining connection with these presystemic issues is essential to the project of providing a basis for understanding the world we live in. For philosophical deliberations to lose their bearing upon the issues that can be posed in the presystemic lingua franca of human experience would be to become *irrelevant* to the aims of the enterprise.

In its explanatory endeavors, philosophy must keep in touch with the empirical domain of ordinary experience from which its issues ultimately emerge. And to connect with these experience-oriented questions of science and quotidian life, we must keep in contact with the concepts in whose terms they are posed. Of course, as its work gets well under way, philosophy eventually becomes increasingly specialized and technical. It turns to issues needed to address further issues themselves arising out of those critical concerns. And so it distances itself from the concepts in whose terms we discuss our prephilosophical experience of things and only talks about matters required for talking about matters needed for talking about such things. At the level of doctrine—of contentions and answers—there is an increasing remoteness and thus little if any overlap between the discourse of technical philosophy and that of ordinary life. But at the level of question resolution, some thread of substantive linkage, some filiation of relevancy to our presystematic concerns, must always be present. The relevance of philosophy as a source of useful insight into the problems regarding the world we live in hinges crucially on this connection with the familiar world of our experience, on this realistic intent to deal—in the final analysis—with the issues we ordinarily encounter in experience.

But one certainly does not want to maintain this sort of conceptual conservatism in science, so why should the situation be so different in philosophy? For the simple and sufficient reason that in philosophy it is *understanding* pure and simple that is of prime concern to us (gaining insight with respect to our presystematic questions), while the characterizing concerns of science is very different, something that lies in the range of praxis in focusing on the issues of successful prediction and interaction or cognitive and operational *control*. This difference between our "merely epistemic" and our "largely practical" concerns is of paramount significance in amounting for the difference between the position of the philosopher and that of the scientist. (It explains, for example, why in quantum physics one is perfectly happy—and perfectly entitled—simply to turn one's back on the principles of our ordinary, everyday conception of the world's modus operandi, something that the philosopher is simply not in a position to do.)

There is, of course, the prospect of ceasing to bother about those presystematic concepts. A theoretician of "enlightenment"—or of consciousness elevation—may indeed urge us to abandon those everyday concepts as somehow misguided and misleading. Such a step could perhaps be urged on grounds of shifting our ideas onto a less conservative, more sophisticated plane. But it could certainly not be taken in an effort to persuade us to improve the practice of philosophy and to help us to engage in its pursuit in a more rigorous and cogent way. For in abandoning those presystematic concepts we also take the more radical course of abandoning philosophy itself, seeing that the mission-definitive questions of the enterprise are formulated in their terms.

To be sure, the radical prospect of simply abandoning philosophy opens up—a prospect which skeptics have urged since classical antiquity (for a more recent version, see Rorty 1982). But this option has a high price. The fact is that we have a very real and material stake in securing viable answers to our questions as to how things stand in the world we live in. In situations of cognitive frustration and bafflement we cannot function effectively as the sort of creature nature has compelled us to become. Confusion and ignorance—even in such "theoretical" and "abstruse" matters as those with which philosophy deals—yield psychic dismay and discomfort. The old saying is perfectly true: Philosophy bakes no bread. But it is also no less true that we do not live by bread alone. The physical side of our nature that impels us to eat, drink, and be merry is just one of its sides. Homo sapiens requires nourishment for the mind as urgently as nourishment for the body. We seek knowledge not only because we wish, but because we must. The need for information, for knowledge to nourish the mind, is every bit as critical as the need for food to nourish the body. Cognitive vacuity or dissonance is as distressing to us as hunger or pain. We want and need our cognitive commitments to comprise an intelligible story, to give a comprehensive and coherent account of things. Bafflement and ignorance—to give suspensions of judgement the somewhat harsher name they deserve—exact a substantial price.

The quest for cognitive orientation in a difficult world represents a deeply practical requisite for us. That basic demand for information and understanding presses in upon us and we must do (and are pragmatically justified in doing) what is needed for its satisfaction. Knowledge itself fulfills an acute practical need. This is where philosophy comes in, in its attempt to grapple with our basic cognitive concerns. The impetus to philosophy lies in our very nature as rational inquirers: as beings who have questions, demand answers, and want these answers to be as cogent as the circumstances allow. Cognitive problems arise when matters fail to meet our expectations, and the expectations of rational order is the most fundamental of them all. The fact is simply that we must philosophize; it is a situational imperative for a rational creature such as ourselves.

Philosophy thus cannot simply abandon these prephilosophical everyday-life concepts that have emerged to reflect our experience. Its need to retain them militates powerfully on behalf of standardism, for those concepts and categories are deeply entrenched in our view of how things normally go in the world. There is no viable alternative to accommodating the presuppositional needs of our everyday concepts in the deliberations of philosophy. Given the origin and nature of its questions, philosophy just cannot avoid coming to terms with the commitment of our concepts to the ordinary and normal course of things as experience presents it to us.

THREE

Standardism and the Theory of Knowledge

SYNOPSIS

(1) Standardism provides an effective way of resolving various well-known difficulties encountered by the classical view of knowledge as true justified belief. (2) An empiricist approach to meaningfulness provides another illustration of the epistemic utility of standardism. (3) In general, a standardistic approach to epistemology offers substantial advantages.

1. An Illustration: The Gettier Problem Sidelined

The idea of construing philosophical generalizations standardistically may appear strange at first sight since this is certainly not how philosophers, traditionally intent on universality and necessity, have usually thought of their generalizations. Nevertheless, much is to be said for such an approach. Let us consider some concrete examples, beginning with one taken from the theory of knowledge. (This chapter's line of thought was initially discussed in Rescher 1991, 59–74.)

Since the time of Plato's *Theaetetus* (201c ff.), a prominent role has been played in the history of philosophical epistemology by the doctrine at issue in the following thesis:

(**T**) Knowledge is true justified belief: Someone knows that *P* just exactly when a belief that *P* is both true and provided with a suitable justificatory account.

After all, we cannot say of a false proposition that someone knows it to be so: "*X* knows that *p*, but *p* is not true" is clearly untenable (although its qualified cousin "*X thinks* he knows that *p*, but *p* is not true" is obviously not). Again, we would not acknowledge that *X knows* that *p*—no matter how firmly *X* believes it—if this individual lacks good reason to justify the belief (let alone if all the information at his disposal actually points the other way). Thus **T** seems in order. Nevertheless, as an example of Bertrand Russell's indicates, there are convincing counterexamples to **T** which clearly indicate the untenability of this otherwise plausible generalization (see the opening discussion of Russell 1912). Consider the case of a person who believes *Q*-or-*R* but does so because (i) she has sound justification for believing *Q* (and thus, a fortiori, for believing *Q*-or-*R*), although *Q* is in actual fact false, while nevertheless, (ii) *Q*-or-*R* is indeed true, albeit only because *R* is true, which our subject has no reason whatever to believe (and may even explicitly reject). In such a case, where the basis of a belief's justification and the basis of its truth are entirely out of alignment with one another, we would certainly not say that the person *knows* the item at issue, despite its status as a true justified belief.

Counterexamples of this sort were made prominent on the contemporary epistemological agenda by an influential paper of Edmund Gettier's (1963), which set afoot a diversified effort to repair or replace **T** through the addition of various further qualifying and complicating provisos—for example, that the justification at issue is provided specifically by factors capable of guaranteeing the truth of the belief. (For a sampling of the resultant literature, see Roth and Gallis 1970; for a detailed survey of the controversy, complete with bibliography, see Shope 1983.) And so, epistemologists have in recent years embarked on a seemingly endless series of ever more elaborately convoluted revisions of **T**, introducing epicycle upon epicycle of further complication to meet ever more sophisticated counterexamples that bring to light flaws in the earlier proposals. For, on traditional principles, a single false instance of course falsifies a generalization, so that a solitary valid counterinstance refutes a general thesis in one decisive blow. A strictly universal generalization that is counterexampled must in consequence either be abandoned or revised.

A standardistic approach alters the situation drastically. For when an epistemological standardism is adopted, we construe the relationship between knowledge and true justified belief not as a *definition* but as a (merely standardistic) generalized linkage:

Standardly, knowledge is true justified belief.

And *this* generalization is perfectly in order; it is not only plausible but largely unproblematic.[1] It is thus clear that the **T**-annihilative strategy of Russell and Gettier will *not* work in the context of an epistemological standardism that proposes to interpret such epistemological generalizations in a standardistic way.

To see this more vividly, let us return to basics and analyze the source of the difficulty. Clearly and pretty much conceded on all sides, for *X* to know that *P*, three conditions must be fulfilled:

i. *P* is indeed true. (One cannot actually *know* a falsehood; one can only *think* that one knows it.)
ii. *X* believes/accepts that *P*. One cannot be said to know a fact—in the overt, explicit sense of "knowledge-that" which is here at issue—if one does not acknowledge is truth.

---

1. It is not always easy to *present* the considerations that justify one's knowledge in anything like their full scope. When I am pressed to substantiate my (correct) claim to know that *maison* is French for *house*, I can do little better than "That's what I learned in school and recall having got on with all these years." But that is good enough "for all practical purposes," which is exactly the point.

iii. *X's* acceptance of *P* is appropriately grounded in the facts of the situation: The factors that ensure *P's* being true play an appropriate part in the rationale for *X's* acceptance of *P.* That is, point (ii) must be appropriately grounded in point (i).

These conditions qualify as necessary and also—puzzle cases posing recherché problems apart—as sufficient.

Now, in the normal and ordinary circumstances of the human cognitive condition, (i) and (ii) carry the whole weight in knowledge situations, and (iii) comes free of charge—because that is in fact how the matter normally stands. Moreover, on a standardistic reading of the generalization those marginal puzzle cases are put aside. Thus, on a standardistic construction, the **T**-thesis is perfectly appropriate, seeing that all those exceptions (optical illusions, and so on) can be consigned to the remote regions of the abnormal.

Accordingly, subject to a standardistic construction of **T,** the counterexamples at issue in the critique of the classic inception of knowledge lose their bite. For now the existence of certain types of exceptions—such as cases exhibiting the aforementioned disconnection between the grounds for a claim and its truth—will be neither surprising nor fatal to an acceptance of **T** in its standardized construction. The entire discouraging and convoluted post-Gettier dialectic of introducing ever more complex epicycles into successive reformulations of **T** in the attempt to block ever more refined and complex counterexamples is aborted at the very outset. Once we approach epistemology from the angle of standardism, **T** becomes an unproblematically acceptable contention, able to dispense with the elaborate efforts that have been lavished on its revision in the Gettier-inspired literature. (Or rather, more generously, one now can and should reconstrue this literature in a constructive light as a potentially instructive attempt to map out the region of the exception categories that are at issue. One family of exceptions, for example, turns on the lack of a *causal* connection between the true facts at issue and the obtaining of the grounds that consitute the rationale of the agent's belief. See Shope 1983 for details.) This example concretely illustrates the utility of a recourse to standardism in epistemology.

2. Another Illustration: An Empiricist View of Meaningfulness

An approach of much the same format could also be used to reinvigorate the empiricist criterion of meaning espoused by the logical positivism of the 1920–1950 era. According to this positivistic standard, a fact-purporting statement is meaningful (informatively viable) if it is possible, in principle, for it to be supported or counterindicated by experientially accessible data.[2] In the subsequent philosophical literature this thesis too was undermined by a series of (successively complex) counterexamples that undermined its tenability (see Hempel 1965). But if the empiricist criterion of factual meaningfulness is once again reconstrued as providing not a *definition* but a standardistically construed *generalization* about the matter ("Meaningful factual statements can normally be confirmed or disconfirmed on the basis of observational evidence"), then the proposed sorts of criticism would simply be beside the point, for there is little difficulty with the idea that, in normal circumstances and ordinary cases, factually meaningful contentions are potentially vulnerable to contrary evidence.

To be sure, the positivistic empiricism at issue would now sacrifice much of its critical bite since the thesis at issue is no longer available for service as an automatic guillotine able to kill of as factually meaningless those statements that resist straightforwardly empirical verification. It would nevertheless still provide a useful dialectical resource for allocating the burden of proof against fact-

2. The "in principle" carries an important burden here. For in the case of historical statements, for example, we clearly cannot return to the past. But we can, of course, discover present traces of past occurrences, as with tree rings or the radiation "echo" left by the "big bang" that gave birth to our cosmos.

purporting theses that defy empirical testing. For anyone who sought to maintain an evidence-impervious contention would now have to assume the discomfiting obligation of consigning it to some authentic exception category. Standardism clearly militates for an empiricist/verificationist approach to meaning, since factual statements standardly function under experiential controls that are crucial alike to their meaning and their meaningfulness.

3. Advantages of Epistemic Standardism

Epistemic standardism as a general policy operative across the board would consist in implementing the following principle:

(**S**) General epistemic theses are always to be construed in the standardistic (rather than strictly universalistic) mode.

In line with this principle, epistemological theses of the format "The *A*s are (are not) *B*s" are to be interpreted as saying, "Standardly, normally, ordinarily: *A*s are (are not) *B*s." This doctrine takes the line that epistemology is an inquiry whose generalizations cannot lay claim to strict universality but have to be construed in the standardistic, exception-admitting mode.

And there is much to be said for such a view. After all, given the complexity of the phenomena at issue, strictly universal generalizations that are unproblematically acceptable are very hard to come by in epistemology. But once we shift to standardistically construed generalizations, the matter stands differently. A profusion of tenable generalizations now becomes available: "People understand what they are told" (for clearly, they *ordinarily* do so), "We remember facts of crucial importance to ourselves" (for clearly this is *normally* so), "People are more confident of what they know than of what they merely surmise" (for clearly, this is so as a rule). Most such epistemic generalizations admit of occasional exceptions in ways that are readily understandable. But they are true almost always—and indeed always "in normal circumstances" and "when other things are equal." Such informative epistemic generalizations cry out for a standardistic interpretation. The domain of performative self-contradictions is another case in point. Here we find statements such as that made by the person who shouts, "I never raise my voice," or—more interestingly—the person who declares, "Everything I say is false." As soon as we construe such statements in the standardistic sense (subject to the proviso "In the normal course of things. . .") all is well and the element of paradox vanishes.

To be sure, some rigidly universal generalizations doubtlessly obtain in epistemology. For example, one would clearly not want to give a merely standardistic reading to self-applicative epistemic generalizations that happen to be true (or false) on strictly logico-conceptual grounds—such as the principle, already discussed, to the effect that "All statements that are *known* to be true are indeed true." But epistemological standardism is comfortably situated to accommodate this situation. For true to its own principles, its thesis "Generalizations about knowledge are only acceptable in a standardistic construction," itself being an epistemological thesis, must be interpreted as falling within its own scope. It too should therefore be interpreted standardistically and is thus perfectly compatible with the existence of rigidly universal generalizations of the sort illustrated by the "analytic" (i.e., meaning-explicative) principle of the aforementioned example.

The advantages of epistemic standardism are thus clear. It relieves the theory of knowledge of commitment to the impossible task of fitting the endlessly varied and complex phenomena at issue in our customary ways of talking and thinking about knowledge into the procrustean bed of totally unexceptionless universality. On standardistic principles, epistemology becomes a venture in clarifying the conception of knowledge actually at issue in the cognitive ground rules that prevail in the normal or usual course of things. As a more "realistic," epistemologically less absolutistic doctrine, standardism transposes those overblown classical epistemological theses into a more plausible and tenable format in a way that contributes substantially to their viability. The diversity and complexity of the phenomena no longer impedes the prospect of achieving tenable generalizations about them, and the oversimplifications inherent in our everyday knowledge no longer condemn to falsity the generalizations articulated in its terms.

FOUR

Standardism and Ethics

SYNOPSIS

(1) Moral luck affects human affairs in such a way that the lives we actually lead—encompassing the actions we actually perform—may just not reflect the sorts of persons we really are from the standpoint of morality. Only in normal circumstances, when things run their ordinary course, will one's moral record *reflect one's moral* nature. *(2) This does not mean, however, that the evaluative principles of morality are somehow deficient; rather, it means that they should be construed standardistically, subject to the supposition that things go normally. (3) The sensible construction of the general rules and principles of morality thus effectively demands a standardistic approach. A viable ethic of general rules cannot be implemented without a standardistic perspective that is focused upon "the accustomed course of things." (4) Kant's principle that "ought" implies "can" affords a prime example of an ethical principle that demands a standardistic in terpretation. (5) The interaction of epistemological and ethical considerations also indicates that a standardistic epistemology is required to operate an ethics that encompasses our moral obligations as generally understood. (6) Moreover, the ethically oriented view of people that we employ in everyday life—*

which insists on seeing people as persons and free agents—is predicated in a standardistic approach.

1. Moral Luck

The case for a standardistic approach to philosophical issues is greatly strengthened by examining the implications of the role of luck in matters of morality. For example, consider the case of the lucky villain who burglarizes his grandfather's house when the latter is on a long journey. Unbeknownst to him, however, the old gentleman has meanwhile died and made him his heir. The property he "steals" is thus his own; legalistically speaking, he has in fact done nothing improper—an undeservedly benign fate has averted the wrong his actions would otherwise have committed. In his soul or mind—in his intentions—he is unquestionably a wicked thief, but in actual fact he is guiltless of any wrongdoing, given the postulatedly accurate description of his act as one of "taking something that belongs to oneself."

By contrast, consider the plight of the hapless benefactor. To do a friend a favor, he has undertaken to safeguard her car during her absence on a long journey. At about the expected time of the friend's return, the car is reclaimed by her scheming identical twin of whose existence our good-natured helper had no inkling. With all the goodwill in the world he has—by a bizarre act of unhappy fate—committed the misdeed of giving one person's entrusted property over to another. In intention, he is as pure as the driven snow but in actual fact he has fallen into wrongdoing. (Compare Nagel 1979, chap. 2; see also Williams 1982, chap. 2, and Richards 1986.)

Cases of this sort illustrate how particular actions of a certain moral status can fail to be "true to form" because of the intervention of fortuitous circumstances. It was, in fact, considerations of just this sort that initially led Kant to put such moral accidents on the agenda of ethical theorizing. For him, they furnish a decisive indication that consequentialism will not do—that we must assess the moral status of actions on the basis not of their actual *consequences*, but on the basis of their *intentions*. As Kant saw it, one's *moral* status and condition—as well as the moral quality of one's acts—are to be determined with reference to the maxims that represent what one wittingly *tries* to do and not by actual outcome, by what it is that, as things eventuate, one actually manages to do. Much can be said for this Kantian view. But it also has its problems. To see just how the land lies, let us first consider how luck can enter into the operation of moral character traits.

Character traits—moral ones included—are dispositional in nature; they are a matter of how people *would* act in certain circumstances. For example, candor and generosity represent morally positive inclinations to support the interests and needs of others—dishonesty and distrust, negative ones. Note that a person can be saved from the actual consequences of malign dispositions by lack of opportunity. In a society of adults—in a mining camp, say, or on an oil rig—the child molester has no opportunity to ply his vice. Again, the very model of dishonesty can cheat no one when, like Robinson Crusoe, he lives alone, shipwrecked on an uninhabited island.

Perhaps all of us are to some extent in this sort of position—moral villains spared only through fortunate circumstances from discovering our breaking point or "learning our price." Perhaps only the lack of opportunity saves most of us from overt villany. As Schopenhauer somewhere observed, the Lord's Prayer petition, "Lead us not into temptation," could be regarded as a plea for matters to arrange themselves so that we need never discover the sorts of people we really are.

After all, from the moral point of view, how people *think*—how they are disposed to deliberate and decide about matters of action—counts every bit as much as what they actually manage to do. The person who is prevented only by the lack of opportunity and occasion from displaying cupidity and greed still remains an avarious person at heart and (as such) merits the condemnation of those right-thinking people who are in a position actually to know this to be so—if such there be. Morality involves more than action and outcome.

The moral status of people as agents is a matter of the "interior" dimension of their intentions, dispositions, and inclinations; it is, in significant measure, a matter of the mindset that determines how "they would act if." Of course, given the difficulties of epistemic access we have no choice but to form our judgments of people inductively on the basis of what we observe them to say and do. But such behavioral data constitute mere *evidence* when the moral appraisal of human agency is at issue. The "morally lucky" villain is not *morally* lucky (by hypothesis, he is a villain); he is lucky only in that his reprehensible nature is not *disclosed*. The difference here is, in the final analysis, not moral but epistemic; it is a matter of not being found out, of "getting away with it." It is precisely because both one's *opportunities* for morally relevant action and (unfortunately for strict utilitarianism) the *actual consequences* of one's acts largely lie outside of one's own control that they cannot appropriately serve as determinants of one's positions in the eyes of morality. Most recent discussions of "moral luck" fail to appreciate that the outcome-distorting good luck of the opportunity-deprived immoralist appertains not to his *moral status* but merely to his *moral reputation*.

Of course, the point cuts both ways. The virtuous person can be preempted from any manifestation of virtue by uncooperative circumstance. Here is the moral hero primed for benevolent self-sacrifice, prepared at any moment to leap into the raging flood to save the drowning child. But fate has staged the drama in an arid and remote oasis, as lacking in drowning children as Don Quixote's Spain lacked authentic damsels in distress. To be sure, we would be unlikely to *recognize* this heroism—in either sense of the term. On the one hand, we would be unlikely to *learn* of it. An on the other, even if evidence did come our way, we could be ill advised to *reward* it in the absence of circumstances that brought it into actual operation (if only because we would not be firmly confident that it is actually strong enough to prevail when there is actual need for its manifestation).

Accordingly, the role of luck in moral affairs has the consequence that the lives we actually lead, encompassing all the actions we actually perform, need not in fact reflect the sorts of persons we really are. But, of course, while this is so, it is not so *normally.* In the usual and ordinary course of things, the circumstances of life are sufficiently varied and complex to offer us ample opportunity to "show what we are made of" and manifest ourselves morally as we indeed are. Life's complexities will generally provide ample scope for showing our true colors and bringing our latent and manifest selves into due coordination. An so standardism comes upon the scene to make the path of morality go straight.

2. Moral Standardism

Does the role of luck in the moral scheme of things mean (as Kant thought) that morality is not of this world—that moral appraisal demands recourse to an inaccessible noumenal order wholly outside this morally askew empirical sphere of ours? Surely not!

We must in general form our moral judgements not on the basis of the situation prevailing *transcendentally* in an inaccessible noumenal realm, but rather on the basis of the most prosaic of all suppositions: that things happen as they *normally and ordinarily* do, that matters take the sort of course that it is only plausible to expect.

Moral evaluation as we actually practice it generally reflects the *ordinary* course of things. Ordinarily, breaking and entering is a wicked thing to do. Ordinarily, leaving one's post to help someone in dire need is a good thing. Ordinarily, driving drunk creates hazards for others. Ordinarily, mendacious people cause pain when they scatter lies about themselves. Ordinarily, people ultimately get to manifest their true colors. Moral appraisals are *standardized* in being geared to the situation of the ordinary run of things.[1] Admittedly luck, be it good

1. To be sure, a standardistic approach to ethics should itself be viewed in the relaxed spirit of standardism. It is perfectly compatible with the idea that *some* ethical precepts obtain in a rigidly universal way (for example, "Do not mislead others just for the fun of it").

or bad, can intrude in such a way as to prevent matters from running in the tracks of ordinariness. And then things go awry as far as the moral dimension is concerned. Moral acts that normally lead to the good can issue in misfortune—or the reverse. But that is just "tough luck." It does not—or should not—affect how matters stand at the level of moral appraisal.

People who drive their cars home from an office party in a thoroughly intoxicated condition, indifferent to the danger to themselves and heedless of the hazards they are posing for others, are equally guilty in the eyes of *morality* (as opposed to *legality*) irrespective of whether they kill someone along the way. Their transgression lies in the very fact of their playing Russian roulette with people's lives. Whether they actually kill someone is simply a matter of luck—of accident and sheer statistical haphazard. The *law* treats these cases differently—and for very good reasons. But the *moral* negativity is much the same one way or the other, even as the moral positivity is much the same one way or the other for the person who bravely plunges into the water in an attempt to save a drowning child. Regardless of outcome, the fact remains that, in the ordinary course of things, careless driving puts people's lives at risk unnecessarily and rescue attempts improve their chances of survival. As the need for a shift from act-utilitarianism to rule-utilitarianism illustrates, what matters for morality is the *general tendency* of actions rather than their actual results under the invariably unforeseeable circumstances of particular cases.

One recent writer flatly denies this:

> Whether we succeed or fail in what we try to do [in well-intentioned action] always depends to some extent on factors beyond our control. This is true of . . . almost any morally important act. What . . . [is accomplished] and what is morally judged is partly determined by external factors. However jewel-like the good will may be in its own right, there is a morally significant difference between actually rescuing someone from a burning building and dropping him from a twelfth story window while trying to rescue him. (Nagel 1979, 25)

The difference Nagel speaks of is indeed present. But it is no more than the product of a lack of specificity in describing the case. Preeminently, we need to know *why* it was that our rescuer dropped the victim. Was it from carelessness or incompetence or a sudden flash of malice? Or was it because despite all due care on his part, Kant's "unfortunate fate" intervened and a burnt-out timber collapsed, pitching him to that window. If so, then Kant's assessment surely prevails.[2] Where a moral

2. "Even if it should happen that, by a particularly unfortunate fate or by the niggardly provision of a stepmotherly nature, this [good] will should be wholly lacking in power to accomplish its purpose, and if even the greatest effort should not avail it to achieve anything of its end, and if

agent's success or failure is differentiated only and solely by matters of pure luck there is patently no reason for making different *moral* appraisals one way or the other.[3]

This Kantian idea goes back to the Greek tradition. The Greek moralists were generally attracted to the following line: How *happy* we are will in general be a matter of accident. *Hêdonê* is chancy business; pleasure is bound to depend on chance and fortune, that is, on the fortuitous opportunities that luck places at our disposal. When fate

there remained only the good will (not as a mere wish but as the summoning of all the means in our power), it would sparkle like a jewel in its own right, as something that had its full worth in itself" (Kant, 1785, sec. 1, para. 3).

3. To say this is not of course to say that we may not want to differentiate such situations on *nonmoral* grounds—e.g., to reward only *successful* rescues or to punish only *realized* transgressions as a matter of social policy *pour encourager les autres*. Against the no-*moral*-difference view, Williams (1982, 24ff.) deploys the example of the person who abandons a life of service to others in order to nourish a penchant for art—a decision whose moral justification (according to Williams) will ultimately hinge on how good an artist the individual turns out to be, which largely depends not on effort but on talent and creative vision issues at the mercy of nature's allocation over which he has no control. But what earthy reason is there for seeing the *moral* situation of the talented Gauguin as being in this regard different from that of the incompetent Ignaz Birnenkopf and to excuse the former where we would condemn the latter? The impropriety of an abandonment of a moral obligation is not negated by the successes it facilitates on other fronts. Kant's point that the talented and untalented, the lucky and the unlucky, should stand equal before the tribunal of morality is well taken, and Hegel's idea that great people stand above and beyond the standards of morality has little plausibility from "the moral point of view."

treats one adversely enough, one may simply be unable to realize the condition of affective happiness as distinguished from that rational satisfaction (*eudaimonia*) that living virtuously affords. Chance plays a predominant role here; circumstances beyond one's power and indeed one's prevision can be decisive in determining outcomes. But our virtue is something that lies within our own control and thus reflects our real nature. People's affective condition in point of *happiness* lies in the hands of the gods, but one's moral condition in point of *goodness* is something that lies in one's own power.

Here Kant was surely right in following the lead of the Greeks. A viable moral theory has to recognize that a person's moral status as such pivots on responsibility and accordingly is indeed impervious to luck: the goodness of the good act and the good person stands secure from the vagaries of irreducibly contingent and unpredictable outcomes. But Kant's *analysis* of this situation went wrong. If morality prescinds from luck, this is not because morality contemplates the *ideal* situation of a *noumenal* sphere but because morality contemplates the *normal* situation of the *ordinary course of things* in this mundane sphere of our quotidian experience, a course from which the *actual* sequence of events can and often does depart.

Of course, there is good reason for viewing the failed and the successful rescue in a different light. For—by hypothesis—we know of the person who brings the rescue off successfully that she has actually persevered to the end, whereas someone whose efforts were aborted by a mishap might possibly have abandoned them before completion for discreditable motives such as fecklessness, folly, or fear. We recognize that an element of uncertainty pervades all human activities and that an unforeseeable burst of inconstancy or weakness might possibly deflect the agent in the process of performing a worthy act. But if we did somehow know for certain—as in real life we never do—that, barring for circumstances beyond her control, the agent would indeed have accomplished the rescue, then we would have no valid basis for denying moral credit. Our reluctance to award full credit has its grounding in considerations that are merely epistemic and not moral. In this regard, Kant's position is clearly on the right track.

With a little novelistic imagination we can all envision bizarre circumstances in which the exercise of the standard virtues (truth-telling, kindness, and so on) repeatedly produces disastrous effects. But their status as virtues is geared toward the standard course of things—how matters *standardly* and *ordinarily* go in the actual world. Because morality as a functional human institution is anchored in the world's ordinary course of things, heroic action is not a demand of morality but a matter of supererogation. (And it is this, of course, that is the Achilles' heel of Kant's own analysis.)

Examples that illustrate the advantages of the present normalcy-oriented approach over Kant's noumenal perspective are not hard to find. Consider the case of Simon Simple, the well-intentioned but extremely foolish lad who, thinking to cure Grandmother's painful arthritis, bakes her for twenty minutes in the large family oven at 400°F. He labors under the idiotic delusion that prolonged exposure to high temperatures is not only not harmful to people but actually helpful in various ways—curing arthritis among them. Accordingly his *intentions* are nothing other than good. Yet few sensible moralists would give Simon a gold star, for he should know what any sensible person knows: broiling people medium well by prolonged exposure to temperatures of 400°F is bad for them. The fact is that we base our moral judgement on the ground rules of the ordinary case. And so, Simon's good intentions simply do not get him off the hook.

In sum, while the role of luck may be decisive for the actual ultimate *consequences* of our actions, it is not so for their *evaluative status*, be it rational or moral. In the final analysis, we should factor luck out in the process of moral evaluation because in these matters our deliberations are inherently geared to the ordinary course of things, rather than to the luck-sensitive issue of how matters actually turn out. (The discussion of this section draws upon Rescher 1990, chap. 10.)

3. The Need for Standardism in Ethics

The general rules that moralists lay down for the proper management of life—be it in moral or prudential or cognitive contexts—are usually implausible if intended with unqualified universality and should not be construed in this way. We say "Do not deceive people," but that does not necessarily mean that you should betray an important confidence whenever some element of deception is involved in keeping it. We say "Always act justly," but do not mean to endorse thereby that *fiat justitia ruat caelum*—that the abstractly just thing should always be done *come what may*. Such rules are *permeable generalities:* They admit of exceptions, though these exceptions should, of course, be rare, on the one hand, and clearly justifiable, on the other.[4] It is not invariably and inevitably that certain sorts of actions are right (keeping promises) or wrong (betraying confidences), but only as a rule—

4. Among contemporary moralists, Alan Donagan (1977, 71–74) is one of the very few to acknowledge that the usual moral rules embody implicit waivers as regards "unusual and unexpected" exception cases that cannot, in general, be specified fully in advance, and whose existence does not invalidate the rules as such.

in the normal and customary course of things.[5] Exceptional, extraordinary circumstances in which those rules and regulations of ethics cannot be applied in a rigid, automatic way can always arise. Compare the situation regarding prudence. It is certainly *possible* for people who throw prudence to the winds to succeed in life through good luck alone, such as by winning a lottery or stumbling upon a treasure trove. But that is not how things normally work; in the normal course of things people have to exert effort to secure their livelihood. And just as the ordinary rules and principles of prudence are geared standardistically to the normal course of things, so are the rules and principles of morality.

In giving practical and ethical advice we generally use formulations that are heavily committed to implicit standardistic qualifications. We say to the child "Do not talk to strangers," but do not mean thereby to exclude asking help from a police officer when the child is lost. We endorse the moral injunction "Do not kill people," but do not thereby intend automatically to enjoin the executioner or the soldier from their deadly work. Of course, one

5. This situation is altered if we take the question-begging step of describing the "sort of action" at issue in a morally tendentious way—e.g., by speaking of *murder* instead of *killing* or of "hurting someone solely for your own pleasure" instead of simply omitting that prejudicial addendum.

could build some (at any rate) of the standardistic qualifications explicitly into the explicit formulation of this injunction: "Do not murder" = "Do not kill anyone *unjustifiably*," and "Do not talk to *inappropriate* strangers." But, as the patently question-begging nature of such formulations indicates, this explicitness is spurious since we have no generally effective way of delineating the range of cases at issue. In any case, this is not in actual fact how we generally proceed. For the most part we formulate our injunctions with an overt and memorable austerity and generality, leaving the limits of their application unspecified, to be filled in by the common sense and good judgment that people generally acquire in the course of their experience as they come to know the sorts of exception categories at issue. (The fact that the line cannot be drawn with surgical precision serves to make ethics the complex business it is.)

Consider any everyday-life concept that also has philosophical interest and relevance—the ethically laden notion of a promise, for example. The question of exactly what sorts of actions and declarations constitute making a promise is far from simple, although it is perfectly clear that *promising* to meet someone at a certain place and time (making an appointment) carries with it various ethical implications, with all its ramifications into the domain of dishonesty and discourtesy. Clearly much (thought not all) hinges on the local customs, that is, the social ground rules of a culture. Anglo-Americans time their appointments to within a range of minutes, while in a Hispanic culture this timing is far more flexible so that the discourtesy of unpunctuality is something quite different in the two settings. The issue of just exactly how the idea of promising operates—how "promises" are made and received, how they are intended and understood—is a crucial issue, and one that is critically reflected in the locally normal and accustomed course of things. And so, the issue of just how and where duty and obligation enter upon the scene—what constitutes promise keeping and promise breaking—is a deeply standardistic issue. The abstract and idealized ethical principle, "Promises should be kept," is safe and secure as such. But the contextual issue of normalcy plays a crucial role here, so that a standardistic approach is very much in order.

Again, consider such widely acknowledged principles of moral philosophy as the following:

- A person who is responsible for an action is also responsible for its consequences.
- A person is responsible for an action only if this individual could have acted so as to produce different results in the circumstances at issue.

Once again, exception cases can arise here. In the first case, we have the problem of consequences that not only could not have been foreseen but which, as "mere flukes" of some sort, actually go against anything that could plausibly have been anticipated. In the second case, we have the problem of the person who freely chooses one alternative totally ignorant of the fact that all the other alternatives were in fact blocked by circumstances beyond his or her control. (To take an example going back to John Locke, think of someone who freely decides to remain in a room, blissfully unaware of actually being locked in.) All such problems clearly relate to "abnormalities," that is, to unusual, extraordinary cases lying outside the range of conditions that standardly prevail. A moral theory incorporating such principles as the preceding cries out for a standardistic interpretation, seeing that a sensible and defensible ethic of general rules cannot be operated without being geared to a standardistic perspective that is focused upon "the usual course of things."

4. Does "Ought" Imply "Can"?

"Every person willing and able to work *ought* to have a job." Right—no question about it. But whether they all *can* do so depends on the state of the economy. "Everyone *ought* to have enough to eat." True. But whether we all *can* do so depends on how many of us there are on the planet. Clearly an *ought* does not in general suffice to assure a *can*.

But what if specific human acts are at issue, rather than general states of affairs? Does not "X ought to do *A*" entail (or presuppose) "X can do *A*"? To all appearances, this entailment does not work either. You ought not to get unduly upset when a friend lets you down. But perhaps you "just can't help it"—which nevertheless does not really destroy that *ought*.

Suppose you take little Johnny to the zoo. You are careless, and Johnny is reckless. He sticks his leg into a lemur's cage and the critter bites him. Johnny cries and to calm him down you promise to make it stop hurting soon. But you cannot actually do so; anesthesia—let alone a magic wand—just is not available. We have an apory:

- *Ought* implies *can*: whatever you ought to do you actually can do.
- You ought to keep your promises.
- You promised Johnny to make it stop hurting.
- You cannot make it stop hurting.

The four statements are inconsistent. One of them has to be abandoned or modified. The last being a "fact of life," we get a choice among the first three. One could drop the third, subject to the idea that a *genuine* promise exists only where its fulfillment is indeed possible. (Not doubt you ought not to have made that unkeepable promise and perhaps that fact stops the putative promise from being a real one.) This is a convenient but highly implausible principle. Promises can be forced into default by unforeseen future contingencies, but surely the issue of *making* a promise is independent of whether this promise *will*—or even in the light of later unforeseeable developments *can*—be kept. Again, one could, perhaps, drop the second thesis, taking refuge in the idea that it properly ought to read:

> "You ought to keep your promises if (and only insofar as) it is possible for you actually to do so."

If we take this line of cutting the *ought* rather than the *promise* itself back to what ultimately proves to be feasible, then we do indeed save "ought" implies "can"—but only by way of the trivializing equation *ought* = *ought insofar as you can*, which is, all too clearly, of very dubious appropriateness. (After all, getting oneself into a fix where doing so becomes infeasible does not necessarily terminate one's obligation to keep a promise.) The least problematic course is (or seems to be) to dispense with that first thesis and abandon the idea of an automatic transition from *ought* to *can*.

It is far from clear, after all, that we *can* do everything that we ought (morally) to do. We *ought* to forget old wrongs, to rejoice at the good fortune of people we dislike, to forgive our enemies. But it is far from clear that we actually can do so except perhaps in the trivial sense of *logical* possibility. Psychologically, this sort of thing may be more than we can bring ourselves to do. But that of course does not get us off the hook of that *ought*.

Consider a somewhat different situation. You borrow $100 from Smith, promising to return it at a certain designated time. You have (just) sufficient funds to repay Smith, and near the appointed hour you are enroute to Smith's house to do so. But on the way, you are mugged and the money is stolen. Seemingly we have a clash:

- *Ought* implies *can*.
- You ought to repay Smith.
- You cannot repay Smith.

Again the last statement of this inconsistent triad is simply a "fact of life," so we have to choose between the first two. We thus confront the alternatives of replacing the first statement by

- *Ought* ought to carry *can* in its wake, but sometimes it just does not.

or replacing the second by

- You ought to repay Smith, but only insofar as you can actually manage to do so.

The second route to consistency restitution is deeply problematic. For if "ought" implied "can"—if feasibility *automatically* curtailed obligation—then there would be an inner inconsistency to saying:

"He ought to be mindful of that infirm pedestrian crossing the road in front of his car, but he just cannot, being too drunk."

But there is clearly no inconsistency here.

It lies in the logic of the situation that we will have "ought" implies "can" iff "cannot" implies "need not"—that is, iff incapacity annihilates obligation. And this it surely does not do in any automatic, across-the-board way. For here the crucial question is: What is the nature of that incapacity. How did it come into existence?

The sentry on duty cannot challenge the intruder because he drank himself into insensibility; the soldier cannot join his mates on the march because he shot himself in the foot; the debtor cannot repay the debt because he gambled the money away. At least in cases where an incapacity is self-generated for reasons of one's own conveniences and wishes, surely no one would say that the agent's obligations have been annihilated through this fact. We would surely say something like, "The agent ought to perform these actions, although—regrettably and quite wrongly—he has put himself into a position of not being able to do so." "You ought to honor your obligations" does not transmute into "You ought to honor your obligations insofar as the circumstances allow," because we are entitled to go on to inquire why it is that you find yourself in those fulfillment-inhibiting circumstances.

Only the most unrealistically lenient among us would restructure the obligation claim at issue so as to readjust it to what the agent actually can do. In such cases, the obligation remains intact, the agent's default notwithstanding. Ordinary language recognizes this fact by adding the special marker "by rights" to indicate the extraordinary character of the situation:

"Smith ought by rights to repay Jones, although he regrettably cannot, seeing that he has gambled the money away."

We thus *qualify* "Smith ought to repay Jones" but certainly do not *abandon* it.

As such examples show, distinguishing in this context between ordinary/normal and extraordinary/abnormal situations is advisable. In *ordinary* cases "ought" does indeed imply "can." But in (sufficiently) extraordinary cases "ought" can actually coexist with "cannot"—as the example of the drunken sentry illustrates. For while the ordinary sorts of "cannot" conditions (namely, externally generated incapacities) would indeed get our sentry off the hook of obligation, that extraordinary self-inflicted incapacity just does not do the trick. The "ought"-implies-"can" principle does not hold hard and fast—all across the board. It only obtains *standardistically* with regard to *normal* and *ordinary* cases.

And so while "ought" does not imply "can," it seems appropriate to say that it does imply "*could if all goes well.*" That is, if even under totally favorable conditions there is no feasible way of discharging a putative obligation, then that "obligation" is dissolved as such. If I owe you the money and you die, then my obligation *to repay you* is canceled as such (though, to be sure, the successor obligation *to repay your estate* now comes to the fore.)

The ethical principle of "ought" implies "can" is thus yet another illustration of a philosophical generalization that does not hold in a strictly universally and absolutely exceptionless way, but only obtains standardistically, allowing certain sorts of literally extraordinary exception cases to slip through its net.

5. Morality and Epistemic Standardism

Interestingly, the issue of *ethical* appropriateness is closely interconnected with that of *epistemic* standardism.

Suppose that we are sailing on the open sea on a vacation cruise ship. It is dusk, and the visibility is getting poor. We are strolling along the starboard side of the ship, when suddenly there is a shout, "Man overboard!" Someone grabs a life preserver from the nearby bulkhead and rushes toward the side of the ship. Suddenly, he comes to a stop and hesitates for a while. To our astonishment he turns, retraces his steps, and replaces the life preserver, calmly proceeding step by step as the site of the incident slips away, first out of reach then out of sight. Puzzled and chagrined, we turn to the individual to ask why he broke off the rescue attempt. The response runs as follows, "Of course, throwing that life preserver was my first instinct, as my behavior clearly showed. But suddenly some ideas from my undergraduate epistemology courses came to mind and convinced me that it made no sense to continue." Intrigued, we ask for more details. He responds as follows:

> What do we actually know? All we could see was that something that looked like a human head was bobbing out there in the water. But the visibility was poor. It could have been an old mop or a lady's wig stand. Those noises we took for distant shouts could well have been no more than a surge of water or a pulsing of the engines. There was simply no decisive evidence that it was actually a person out there. And the I remembered William Kingdon Clifford's dictum, "It is wrong always, everywhere, and for anyone, to believe anything upon insufficient evidence." So why act on a belief that there was actually a human being in danger out there, when the evidence for any such belief was clearly insufficient? And why carry out a rescue attempt when you do not believe that somebody actually needs rescuing?

Something has clearly gone wrong here. Whatever sympathy we may have for our misguided shipmate as an epistemologist, we will incline to wonder about his moral competence.

Even if I unhesitatingly accept and endorse the abstract principle that one must try to be helpful to others in situations of need, I am clearly in moral difficulty if I operate on too stringent a standard of evidence in relevant contexts—one which in actual fact will never allow me to enter into an epistemic situation where this principle comes into overt operation—For then I will be systematically precluded from ever actually doing things that, from a moral perspective, I *ought* to do.

To operate in life with *epistemological* principles that impede one in the discharge of "normal" *moral* obligations is to invite justified reproach. Where the interests of others are potentially at risk, we cannot, with moral appropriateness, deploy evidential standards of acceptability of a higher, more demanding sort than those standardly operative in a community of sensible people. At this point, epistemology has moral ramifications. Morality, as we know it, requires a relatively commonsense epistemology for its appropriate implementation. To proceed in ethics in a sensible and defensible way, we must operate on epistemic principles that are themselves committed to an acceptance of "the normal course of things." The interlinkage of ethical with epistemological considerations indicates that a standardistic epistemology is required by any ethics that encompasses our moral obligations as they are generally understood.

An important point is at issue here: Even in ethics, where to all appearances we deal not with the actualities of what is but with normative issues of what should be—that is, with idealizations—our conceptions are actually predicated upon an empirical basis of knowledge or supposition about how things ordinarily go in the world. For since "ought" standardly implies "can," one's *oughts* have to be formulated with some degree of "realism"—some recognition or supposition regarding reality's *can-be's*. This issue of what can be—of what reality's compartments are ample enough to accommodate—is always a matter of experience, of our view of the world's modus operandi—of how its processes go in the normal course of things.

An ethic of rules cannot attune itself flawlessly to the virtually endless complexities of the real world and cannot provide for the endless variation of conceivable circumstances, for then the rule framer would have to do the job not only of the legislators, but of the trial judges as well.[6] If the rules were so complicated, it would become effectively impossible for anyone to *formulate* them, let alone to *learn* them. Our body of moral rules would be of incomparably greater length and complexity than

6. The focus of these remarks upon an ethic of rules should not be construed as suggesting that this is the whole of ethics, that there is no room for an ethic of principles or one of virtues. The discussion is only predicated on the belief that an ethic of rules forms an important *part* of ethics. (How large the share of this part actually is an issue we need not address for present purposes.)

the operating instructions for a battleship or the manual of regulations for operating an airline. Any code of civil or common law devised over the ages would be like a drop in the ocean compared to the manual of morality. This volume of complexity would be altogether fatal to the capacity of the rules to do the sort of job for which a moral code is instituted, since it is a prime function of a moral code to guide people into smooth and mutually beneficial patterns of interrelation with one another. To do the sort of work that is at issue here, the moral rules have to be learnable "at mother's knee." A system of morality (like a system of language) must be something that a person of average intelligence can master in its essentials by the age of seven or eight.

If it were overly complex or sophisticated, a moral code could not survive as a living force in a human community. It could not preserve itself in place through transmission from generation to generation. Its maintenance would have to be the work of a special elite, that is, of trained experts. Its ability to function and to regulate our doings and dealings with one another in the interactions of everyday life would become totally unstruck.

A viable ethic of rules must be a manageably sized family of injunctions of the form "In situations that meet condition *C*, do *A*." The difficulty is that even though doing *A* is appropriate in most cases when condition *C* obtains (or in all *standard* cases when this is so), it is never *always* appropriate. Adverse conditions can always result in a nonstandardness that makes following the rule inappropriate *in a particular case*. No set of learnable rules can possibly take all permutations and combinations of possible adversity into account.

Rules are necessarily generic in character: They can only specify types of obligation. And any given type of obligation can always be overridden in special cases, such as when its default turns out to be the lesser of the evils. Rules can only specify the generalities of action, but particular acts must be performed in concrete circumstances whose ramifications can never be encompassed *in toto* by any set of rules. A system of moral rules that did *not* "oversimplify" matters would through this very fact become unworkable. (This holds, mutatis mutandis, for an ethic of examples and paradigms as well.)

But just where is one to locate the rule in relation to the exceptions? Why have the rule be "Do not kill people" with exceptions in the case of executioners in line of duty, soldiers in wartime, police officers under threat, and so one rather than "Killing people is acceptable except in such-and-such (duly contrived) conditions." The answer in relation to moral issues lies in the matters of values and priorities which, in this case, is the sacredness of (human) life. Moral rules, after all, are not freestanding but are part of a value framework that underlies their legitimation. The rules, in sum, must have a cogent rationale.

Accordingly, all that a moral code can do is provide general guidelines. Moral principles and rules can indeed orient and guide but cannot determine and specify action; they cannot give us detailed instructions for what to do under endlessly complex and varying conditions and circumstances. A moral code has to be substantially less complex than the Code of Justinian or the Napoleonic Code, let alone the maintenance manual for a jet aircraft. All it can do—and all it need do—is give us guidance in ordinary or standard circumstances. The rest it can (and must) leave to people's good sense and understanding of the spirit of the enterprise. The need for and the utility of a viable ethic strongly enjoins a standardistic approach in this domain.

6. A Standardist Approach to Human Beings: People as Free Agents

In 1748, Julien Offray de la Mettrie published in Leiden his startling treatise *Man a Machine (L'Homme machine)*, giving vivid expression to the naturalism that culminated the intellectual ethos of this iconoclastic era of the age of reason. De la Mettrie's contentions may have looked foolish at a time when the most complicated machines were clockworks and windmills but they certainly seem far less so in the present era of electronic "thinking machines" programmed to display "artificial intelligence." Perhaps, then people are no more than machines?

The shock effect of the idea of people as machines lies in the fallacious impression that this circumstance would somehow *change* what people are in fact. For we incline to think that we would thereby be devalued, that human life would cease to be significant. But how does this follow? If one accepts that someone's body consists of chemical elements—mainly water—whose market value is but a few dollars, does that have any implications for her or his value as a *person*? Why should it? The closer one looks, the less apparent the reason.

People sometimes feel themselves threatened by the following line of argumentation:

1. People are machines
2. Machines cannot do X (have feelings, have free will, and so on)

Therefore, people do not do X (have feelings, have free will, and so on).

But to maintain (2) is in effect to beg the question once (1) is asserted. While (2) is indeed acceptable on a standardistic understanding of machines, (1) now does not suffice to yield this conclusion, since the condition of normalcy is (or may well be) lacking at this point. Certainly *typical* machines do not behave in the way envisioned in (2). Yet a human being, even if a machine, is certainly *not* a typical machine, but one that has a "spiritual" dimension of norms, values, purposes, and the like.

The shock value of claiming that people are machines comes from the circumstance that it is all too easy to make the fallacious leap from the contention "People are machines" to the conclusion "People are *typical* machines," imputing to human beings all those features that characterize typical artifactual machines (such as, for example, lack of free will). Of course this no more follows than the far-fetched conclusion "People are *typical* animals" follows from "People are animals." A cautious standardism geared toward the normal and accustomed condition of things comes to the aid of common sense in enabling us to avert such bizarre conclusions.

Even if it were to turn out in the end to be appropriate to categorize Homo sapiens as a machine, this eventuality would flatly fail to dehumanize us. If humans are indeed machines, then they are certainly machines of an extraordinary kind—organic, intelligent, capable of feeling, suffering, loving, and so on. If people are machines then it transpires that machines can do some rather nonmachinelike things. The result of endorsing the view that "People are machines" could revolutionize not only our idea of human beings, but our idea of what it is to be a *machine* as well.

As this example illustrates, a philosophy geared to a standardistic concern for the normal and typical course of things is able to avert an artificiality and unrealism at odds with a sensible treatment of various key philosophical issues. A standardistic approach is congenial to our everyday (non-LaMettriean) conception of persons as freedom-endowed moral agents. Our everyday conception of ourselves is predicated upon commitments geared to a normalized understanding of what a *person* is.

The moral philosopher tells us that *people* (human beings, members of our biological species) are to be regarded as *persons*—intelligent and responsible free agents who consider themselves as such and acknowledge one another in the same light. But this of course overlooks endless complications. Some people are too young for intelligent agency (infants), some too ill or too injured. It is only normally that people control their own actions, and not with invariable necessity. Now consider, in this light, the issue of free will, which is pivotal to moral philosophy through the principle that only free agents are morally responsible for their actions. It is certainly not the case that free agency, and thus morality, would vanish from the world if it turned out that the nature is altogether a theater of materialistic/deterministic causal processes, for it is not determination as such that precludes freedom, but the determination of factors other than those relating to the agent's desires, wishes, preferences, and so on. If there were an "inner determination"—if the agent's actions were the product of the *normal* operation of its own materialistic brain (and not, say, programmed by a posthypnotic suggestion)—then the crucial condition of effective control over one's own actions would still be satisfied. The freedom at issue is not freedom from any and all causal determination, but freedom from both external control and abnormal inner constraint, which is perfectly compatible with an internally operative determination through an agent's own motives and desires. "But what if someone is born with an abnormality in his or her brain that makes him or her compulsive or schizophrenic. Surely one would say that this person's acts are not free—that even though they result from the agent's desires and preferences, these themselves are the mere product of the disease or malfunction at issue." Yes indeed, that may well be what one would say. For what counts as freedom is not *just* a matter of "issuing from the agent's own thought processes" but one of issuing from these processes when they themselves proceed *normally*. (The "norm" at issue here is not a merely locally statistical one; we might be dealing with a society in which schizophrenics preponderate.) It is exactly this reference to the healthy normality of the action-engendering thought processes that is crucial for the issue of free will in its moral dimension.

The crucial fact for present purposes is that our standard, normality-geared approach toward the world we live in enables us to put aside not only the paranoia of worriment about external manipulative agents (deceiving demons, hypnotists, wicked scientists, and so on) but also those various far-fetched responsibility-abrogating inner conditions (brain abnormalities, irrational cravings and the like). A part of what makes us into free rational agents is a healthy state of mind in which we see ourselves in this light, accept one another as such, and envision the world's realities in terms consonant with these policies of ours.

It is not that our commonsense ethic, geared as it is to seeing people as possessors of free will, has somehow refuted metaphysical determinism. The crux is, rather, that on any interpretation of "free agency" worth having, people must count as free agents in the normal and ordinary course of things. Moreover, a moral code must—and is perfectly entitled to—recognize the quotidian realities of this world and thereby to place some reliance on the fact that normally and ordinarily things go well enough for people to be in a position to honor their commitments and discharge their obligations. Such a code can, and must, rely on the fact that reality is by and large benign—that exotic eventuations are the exception, not the rule, in human affairs. Accordingly, the general principles of moral philosophy on the order of "Actions determined by one's own wishes and hopes are free" cry out to be construed in the standardistic mode—this very generalization itself, no doubt, included.

FIVE

Standardistic Ontology

SYNOPSIS

(1) Metaphysical realism invites a standardistic approach to the world's furnishings. (2) A realistic metaphysic calls for a standardistic ontology of experientially knowable objects as we encounter them in the normal and ordinary course of things.

1. Metaphysics and Standardistic Semantics

Standardism also has a useful role to play in the sphere of ontology in providing a natural and efficient resource for conceptualizing the world's furniture. For any sensible and viable realism demands a standardistic approach to the knowability of real things, based on the supposition that our view of them, while full of gaps, can appropriately be rounded out in the "normal" way—that is, in line with our standard conception of the sort of thing at issue. We have little choice but to construe our claims about the nature of experientiable reality in standardistic terms of reference geared to the ordinary course of things as we normally encounter them. Let us consider why this is so.

As we standardly think about things within the conceptual framework of our fact-oriented thought and discourse, *any* real physical object has more facets than it will or indeed could ever manifest in experience. Every objective property of a real thing has consequences of a dispositional character, and these can never actually be surveyed *in toto* because the dispositions that particular concrete things inevitably have endow them with an infinistic aspect that cannot be comprehended within experience. For example, this desk, at which I write, has a limitless manifold of phenomenal features of the type "having a certain appearance from a particular point of view." It is perfectly clear that most of these will never be actualized in experience. Moreover, a thing *is* what it *does;* entity and lawfulness are coordinated correlates—a good Kantian point. This consideration that things demand lawful comportment means that the finitude of experience precludes any prospect of the *exhaustive* manifestation of the descriptive facets of any real things. (This aspect of objectivity was justly stressed in the "Second Analogy" of Kant [1787] 1965, though his discussion rests on ideas already contemplated by Leibniz 1875–1890, vol. 7, 319ff.)

The fact is that physical things, as we standardly conceive them, not only have more properties than they ever *will* overtly manifest, they actually have more than they ever *could* actually manifest, because the dispositional properties of things always involve what might be characterized as *mutually preemptive* conditions of realization. This cube of sugar, for example, has the dispositional property of reacting in a particular way if subjected to a temperature of 10,000° C and of reacting in a certain way if emplaced for one hundred hours in a large, turbulent body of water. But if either of these conditions is ever realized, it will destroy the lump of sugar as a lump of sugar, and thus block the prospect of *its* ever bringing that other dispositional property to manifestation. Although the realization of individual dispositions is possible, their conjoint realization is not; they fail to be mutually *compossible*. Accordingly, the dispositional properties of a thing cannot be manifest *in toto*—not just in practice but in principle.

The existence of this latent and observationally invisible sector of merely dispositional features is a crucial facet of our conception of a real thing. Our objective claims about real things always commit us to more than we can ever determine about them. To say of the apple that its only features are those it *actually* manifests is to run afoul of our conception of an apple. To deny, or even merely refuse to be committed to the claim that it *would* manifest particular features *if* certain conditions came about (for example, that it would have such-and-such a taste if eaten) is to abandon the claim that it is an apple. The process of corroborating the contents inherent in our objective factual claims about anything real is potentially endless, so that such judgements are "nonterminating" in C. I. Lewis's sense (1947, 180–81). This cognitive inexhaustibility of our objective factual claims means that their *content* will always outrun the content of any finite body of *evidence* for making them. G. E. Moore's paradigm of a claim of commonsense realism, "This is a human hand," exemplifies this circumstance. For even this simple assertion has an unending variety of factual consequences ("The hand will not turn into gold if pecked hard by a dodo bird") that we can never fully control by way of actual checking.

As these considerations indicate, the things we think of as actually existing in the world are always conceptualized as having features that transcend experience. Our thought and discourse about real things involves an element of *experience-transcending imputation*, of commitment to claims that go beyond the experientially acquirable information. Yet the rejection of such claims would mean our having to withdraw the thing characterization at issue. To say of something that it is an apple or a stone or a tree is to become committed to claims about it that go beyond the data we have—and even beyond those that we can ever obtain about it.

This, then, is how the conceptual scheme of everyday life regards the real things of the world: as objects endowed with such inherent depth and complexity that the information we acquire never will, and never could, exhaust the realm of pertinent fact. Any claim about the objective features of real things carries us beyond the limits of actual experience. An unavoidable information gap arises that can only be filled in by the supposition that all the "unknowns" stand in the manner a normal arrangement in conformity with the ordinary course of things.

Accordingly, a standardism geared to the way in which we normally conceive of things will play an important part in any metaphysic that is "realistic" in either the philosophical or the everyday sense of the term. A realistic metaphysic of knowable objects requires a standardistic semantics of normal evidential relationships on whose basis finite data authorize evidence-transcending imputations via the presumption that the usual condition of things can be assumed to obtain in the absence of evidence to the contrary.

2. A Standardistic View of Things Lies at the Basis of Cognitive Realism

The standardistic point of view provides a natural approach to the metaphysics of real-world objects. For our thought about the real things of this world presses outward beyond the limits of perception and indeed beyond any and all surveyable boundaries. From finitely many axioms, reason can generate a potential infinity of theorems; from finitely many words, language can exfoliate a potential infinity of sentences; from finitely many data, reflection can extract a potential infinity of items of information. Even with a world of finitely many objects, the process of gaining information about these objects can, in principle, continue without end. One can inquire about their features, the features of those features, and so on. Or again, one can consider their relations, the relations among those relations, and so on. Our various modes of thought—abstraction, imagination, analysis—are inherently ampliative processes. As in physical reflection, where mirror images can reflect one another indefinitely, so mental reflection can go on and on. Given a start, however modest, thought can advance ad indefinitum into new informative terrain.

The number of true descriptive remarks that can be made about any actual physical object is theoretically inexhaustible. Let us take a stone, for example. We can consider its physical features: its shape, its surface texture, its chemistry, and so forth. We may then consider its causal setting: its genesis and subsequent history as well as its functional aspects as relevant to the stonemason, the architect, the landscape gardener, and so on. There is, in principle, no theoretical limit to the different lines of consideration available to yield descriptive truths about a thing, so that the totality of potentially available facts about real things is in principle inexhaustible. The circumstance of its starting out from a finite initial basis does not mean that inquiry need ever run out of impetus (as the example of Shakespearean scholarship seems to illustrate).

All the same, language-bound thought has its limitations. For while every truth must state a fact, it is in principle possible for facts to exist that cannot be stated in any actually available language and thus fail to be captured as truths. It is helpful to introduce a distinction at this stage. If we adopt the standard conception of the matter, then a truth is something to be understood in *linguistic* terms, that is, the representation of a fact through its statement in some actual language. Any correct statement in some extant language formulates a *truth*. (The converse obtains as well: A truth must be encapsulated in a statement and cannot exist without linguistic embodiment.) A *fact*, on the other hand, is not a linguistic entity at all, but an actual circumstance or state of affairs. Anything that can be stated correctly in some possible language presents a fact. (The position at issue thus has no quarrel with Strawson's precept that "facts are what statements (when true) state" [1950, 136]. Difficulty would ensue only if an "only" were inserted.) Facts afford potential truths whose actualization as such hinges on their being given a linguistic formulation. Truths involve a one-dimensional possibilization: They include whatever *can* be stated truly in some *actual* language. Facts, on the other hand, involve a two-dimensional possibilization—they include whatever can be stated truly in some *possible* language. Truths are *actualistically* language-correlative, while facts are *possibilistically* language-correlative. Accordingly, it must be presumed that there are facts that will never be formulated as truths, though it will obviously be impossible to give concrete examples of this phenomenon.[1]

Now propositional knowledge regarding facts (including belief and conjecture) is always a matter of linguistically formulatable information. But we have no alternative to supposing that the realm of facts regarding the real things of this world is larger than the attainable body of statable truth (or purported truth) about them—regardless of whether that "we" is construed distributively or collectively. It is easy to see why this is so. As long as we are concerned with claims formulated in languages

1. Note, however, that if a Davidsonian translation argument to the effect that "if it's sayable at all, then it's sayable in *our* language" were to succeed—though it does not—then the matter would stand on a different footing. It would follow that any possible language can state no more than what can be stated in our own (actual) language. Then the realm of facts (i.e., what is [correctly] statable in some *possible* language) and that of truths (i.e., what is [correctly] statable in some *actual* language) would necessarily coincide. Accordingly, our thesis that the range of facts is larger than that of truths hinges crucially upon a failure of such a translation argument. (See Davidson 1973–1974, and the critique of his position in Rescher 1982, chap. 2.)

of the standard (recursively developed) sort, the number of actually articulated items of information (truths or purported truths) about a thing is always, at any historical juncture, finite. It remains denumerably infinite even over a theoretically endless long run (see Hugley and Sayward 1983). The domain of truth is therefore, in principle, sequentially enumerable but that of fact is not comparably manageable. Reality, as we conceive of it, outruns any such limitation.

To see why this is so, let us begin with the idea that an object *X* is "cognitively inexhaustible" if no finite list of truths about *X* captures the totality of true facts about it. Now it is easy to see that even an infinite list of distinct truths about *X* will fail to capture the totality of pertinent facts. Let the series

$f_1, f_2, f_3, \ldots$

represent a purportedly complete listing of distinct facts about *X*, that is, a supposedly complete serial inventory of them. This listing is, by hypothesis, such that (1) each of its members represents a truth about *X*; and (2) each successive member adds something new, so that, for any *i*,

$\sim(C_i \rightarrow f_{i+1})$, where by definition $C_i = f_1 \,\&\, f_2 \,\&\, \ldots \,\&\, f_i$ and '$\rightarrow$' represents logical implication.

To show that the infinite f_i-list does not manage to register the *totality* of actual fact about *X*, consider the infinite conjunction of all the f_1:

$C_\infty = f_1 \;\&\; f_2 \;\&\; f_3 \;\&\; \ldots .$

This conjunction clearly represents yet another true fact about *X*. Yet, by the aforementioned condition of novelty, this fact itself clearly cannot occur anywhere on the f_i list. So the inventory is not complete after all—contrary to assumption.

This reductio ad absurdum of our hypothesis of enumerative completeness indicates that the facts about a thing are necessarily too numerous for explicit enumeration. Once we recognize that real things are cognitively inexhaustible in that the true facts about them cannot be encapsulated in any finite body of contentions, we must acknowledge that even infinite listings will prove insufficient.

It might be possible, however, to have latent or implicit knowledge of an infinite domain through deductive systematization. After all, the finite set of axioms of a formal system will yield infinitely many theorems. So it might seem that when we shift from overt or explicit to implicit or tacit knowledge, we secure the prospect of capturing an infinitely diverse *implicit* knowledge content within a finite *explicit* linguistic basis. The matter is not so convenient, however. The totality of the deductive consequences that can be obtained from any finite set of axioms is itself always denumerable. The most we can ever hope to encompass by way of deductively implicit containment within a finite basis of truths is a denumerably infinite manifold of truths. Thus as long as implicit containment remains a recursive process, it too can never hope to transcend the range of the denumerable, and so cannot hope to encompass the whole of the nondenumerable range of descriptive facts about a thing. (After all, even within the denumerable realm, our attempt at deductive systematization runs into difficulties. As is known from Gödel's work, one cannot even hope to identify—by any recursive, axiomatic process—all of the inherently denumerable truths of arithmetic.)

As these deliberations indicate, our ontological view of the real things of this world must not be too closely geared to with the way we actually believe or understand things to be. Things *as we know them*—as we keep them tamed in our cognitive domestication—represent no more than our best realizable *estimate* of the nature of the real. We must acknowledge that this may ultimately fail to do justice to the realities at issue unless and until we can presume, as we must, that matters stand normally in that (so to speak) "what we don't know can't hurt us" in the way of destabilization. The provisionality inherent in a standardism of how we normally and ordinarily conceive of things is indispensable to any viable version of a "cognitive realism" which maintained that things more or less are as we deem ourselves to "know" them.

SIX

Standardism and Philosophy of Nature

SYNOPSIS

(1) The stochastic revolution in natural science has replaced the classical, deterministic approach to understanding nature through universal laws of exceptionless generality by ones that proceeds on the basis of statistical principles. Natural science no longer views the world's operations in terms of processes that inevitably lead to predetermined results; rather, it often proceeds probabilistically, in terms of how things stand in the statistical run of things. (2) In dispensing with an uncompromising reliance on rigidly universal relationships, a science of this probabilistic complexion sets the stage for a philosophy of nature that is articulated in standardistic terms. (3) These considerations serve to provide a theoretical rationale for the appropriateness of philosophical standardism.

1. Stage-setting: The Stochastic Revolution and the Role of Chance

The applicability of our scientific "laws of nature" is generally limited to ideal conditions subject to provisos precluding the intrusion of "disturbing factors." Such idealizations block the physical system at issue from external perturbations (see Cartwright 1983 and Hempel 1988). In consequence, we approximate reality through calculations that use such laws in a normalcy-coordinated way—envisioning circumstances where the real situation *approximates* (at least roughly) to those ideal conditions. The applicative implementation of our scientific theories involves a reference to (contextually) normal conditions in a way that evokes the spirit of standardism.

But standardism also has another, even deeper rationale in the philosophy of nature. Discovering the essentially stochastic nature of fundamental microphysical processes has overthrown the older deterministic and necessitarian view of the world that characterized physics in its classical, Newtonian configuration. In the wake of the stochastic revolution in modern physics, philosophers of science, students of the scientific method, and working scientists concerned about conceptual fundamentals have come to occupy themselves more and more with something whose necessity they have acknowledged only grudgingly: a fundamental reexamination of the very meaning of *scientific explanation*. Traditionally, explanation has been understood in terms of subsumption under universal natural laws. The discovery in twentieth-century physics of the extent to which nature is fuzzy and indeterministic in operating on statistical and stochastic principles, however, has engendered a view of scientific explanation prepared to recognize as appropriate explanatory arguments that render the facts at issue *not necessary but merely probable*. (For a detailed and interesting survey of the historical background see Salmon 1989.)

This stochastic revolution has accordingly had profound implications for the very *terms of reference* used in articulating our understanding of the way in which the processes of nature work. It means that we must refrain from propounding principles of description and explanation that purport to show how nature will and must universally and necessarily function. Given the fundamentally random character of natural processes, there are various sectors of nature where it makes no sense to persist in demanding rigid "general principles" of natural necessity that specify—in the manner of classical Newtonian laws—how things must inevitably and invariably work at the level of individual cases and instances. The domain of *stochastic* processes must be reckoned with. Chance and chaos come into their own.

This change has produced a fundamental shift of outlook. In the ordinary physical course of things, thermodynamic systems move from states of greater diversity to states of greater homogeneity. In the ordinary biological course of things, organisms that are more fit produce a more enduring posterity. In the ordinary course of communications transmission, information is lost and not gained—and so on. Our understanding of the world's processes is based not on universal and exceptionless principles of invariable necessity but on a statistically grounded grasp of "how things generally go." We have been impelled to abandon the classical Newtonian necessitarianism of a Kantian a priori natural necessity and universality and to turn, instead, to a stochastic probabilism that is perhaps less rationally tidy but, nevertheless, superior in its capacity to explain satisfactorily the phenomena as we actually observe them. Our understanding of the world we live in has thus come to be predicated on a statistically geared conception of physical law. We now no longer describe the workings of the world in terms of processes that inevitably lead to prespecifiable results but rather view them probabilistically. The consequent diffusion of probabilistic ideas throughout our understanding of natural processes also helps set the stage for a standardistic approach to the theory of nature.

2. A Standardistic Philosophy of Nature

Matters look very different once we abandon the Newtonian program of classical physics enshrined in the necessitarianism of Kant, with its insistence on understanding the world through explanations that stipulate how, on the basis of abstract general principles, things must operate in nature at the level of universality and necessity. When stochastic phenomena enter upon the scene, we can no longer describe the world in terms of how things always go, everywhere and invariably. The descriptive generalizations that encapsulate our scientific picture of nature, and that ultimately provide the basis for a philosophical understanding of the world we live in, have to reflect the general course of things, that is, the normal patterns of natural comportment. The world can now no longer be thought of as the theater of operation of rationally exigent uniformities rooted deeply in the nature of things. Clearly, the shift from classical necessitarianism to the probabilism of a stochastic view of nature invites and encourages a standardistic metaphysics geared to an empirically informed picture of the customary ways in which things work, that is, a standardistic view of things based on an understanding of their normal and usual operations.

Once chance, randomness, and chaos have become significant factors in our picture of reality, it becomes plausible that a philosophy designed to characterize the world's nature should be of a standardistic sort that can no longer be geared to inherently rational abstract general principles. The necessitarian view of nature's modus operandi must yield to one geared to a less rigid, more contingent view of the realities of the statistical record, that is, to how things go in line with an experience-reflective view of the "normal course of events" on the world's stage. Agents operating in a world pervaded by chance have little alternative but to view events on the basis of how they go, normally and ordinarily, within the framework of their experience.

The point that comes to the fore here should be stated with care. It is *not* being maintained that the prominence of probabilistic law and statistical explanation in modern physics is itself standardistic in nature. This would be false since "normalcy" and "the ordinary course of things" play no role whatsoever in contemporary physical science: The probabilistic relationships that underlie explanations in classical statistical mechanics and in quantum statistical mechanics do not represent standardistic generalizations. Rather, the point is that in a world in which chance and chaos play so prominent a role, the nature of human experience is bound to be such that the lessons we can draw from it and the explanatory principles by which we can characterize its bearing on our affairs will have to be of a standardistic sort. In a largely chaotic world, whose descriptive arrangements are not exceptionlessly rigid—not strictly universal in their bearing but reflective of how matters stand generally and in the ordinary course of things—the philosophical theses by whose means we articulate our experience-reflective picture of nature will have to be geared to the usual course of things. The realities of a chance-pervaded world invite and encourage recourse to philosophical standardism.

3. A Rationale for Standardism

The deliberations of this chapter make it possible to articulate the rationale for philosophical standardism in a clear and compact format. Philosophical standardism is not just predicated on an induction from examples; it has a cogent theoretical validation as well. The case for metaphysical standardism has a deep rooting in the physical nature of the world we live in. This validation, in schematic outline, runs as follows:

- The substantiation of philosophical theses calls for discerning the clarificatory (meaning-explicative) relationships among the internally complex (experience-reflective) concepts that are used in formulating the issues of the field.
- Philosophically relevant concepts are experientially grounded. Their internal integrity and viability as meaningful units of communication is predicated on suppositions about the facts. They are, accordingly, fact-laden and always reflect their user's understanding of the world's arrangements.
- The world is chaotic: Its detailed arrangements are not subject to exceptionless rules but generally admit of cases that are deviant and nonconforming. Any adequate grasp of the facts will reflect this circumstance, which renders rigid and rigorously universal relations among concepts

> infeasible. The only ultimately viable generalizations at our disposal in this domain are those geared to the normal course of things as experience presents it to us.

It emerges on this basis that the generalizations suitable for conveying plausible philosophical positions can, in the end, only be maintained on a basis of a limiting qualification to what is the case "standardly, normally, and in ordinary circumstances." The overall line of justificatory reasoning is a straightforward one, rooting in the consideration that our philosophically relevant concepts are fact-coordinated, so that their clarification accordingly demands an empirically informed approach, linked to the world's chaotic realities. For, this means that these empirical linkages are not conceptually airtight; they have to be based on an experientially informed view of the normal course of things. This normality-geared orientation in turn creates a situation when it is only natural that the conceptually based generalizations of philosophy should be construed standardistically.

These deliberations accordingly map out the theoretical considerations that combine to furnish a justificatory rationale for philosophical standardism. They indicate that it is not by accident that this position makes sense in various particular instances and situations, seeing that reasons of basic principle underly the serviceability of this approach to the business of philosophizing. Our philosophical inquiries proceed in a setting where the nature of reality and the nature of our conceptual resources for its characterization conspire to underwrite the suitability of standardism.

SEVEN

Standardism, Reflexivity, and Metaphilosophy

SYNOPSIS

(1) Philosophy is a reflexive discipline: Methodological questions about *the field always fall* within *the field itself. (2) Metaphilosophy—the philosophical study of philosophy itself—being a domain where self-critical and reflexive generalizations are prevalent, thereby constitutes a natural habitat for standardism. (3) In particular, the thesis of epistemic standardism itself can be—and should be—interpreted standardistically. (4) And kindred considerations render a standardistic approach plausible throughout the range of deliberations about human knowledge.*

1. Philosophy as a Reflexive Discipline

Standardism finds its foothold in philosophy because of the chaotic nature of the world. But what about metaphilosophy—the philosophical study of philosophy itself? Surely here the situation is different. Whatever the nature of the world, the situation in philosophy should, after all, be orderly and rational. (Even a theory of inebriation should itself be sober.) Thus if standardism is also to find a foothold in metaphilosophy, it must be through something other than the chaotic complexity of the phenomena. And this is indeed so. The case for standardism in metaphilosophy rests not on chaos but on reflexivity.

Reflexivity is the phenomenon that manifests itself in reflection, that is, in the turning of arrangements inwards upon themselves. The two modes of reflexivity are the *personal* (singular as per him-or-her SELF or plural with our-SELVES) and the *impersonal* (it-SELF). In the former context, people's affairs or actions are referred back to themselves. In the latter context, there are two main versions: (1) the *processual* reflexivity of processes that feed back upon themselves, providing grist for their own mill, so to speak (much as in cognitive psychology the *processes* of inquiry themselves constitute *subjects* of inquiry); and (2) the *semantical* reflexivity of linguistic units (statements, discourses, rules, questions) that, directly or indirectly, refer to themselves—often in paradoxical ways.[1] Specifically, a statement is self-referential when it falls within the scope of its own assertion. (For discussions of reflexivity and references to the literature, see Bart-

1. A nice example of a reflexive rule is afforded by the paradoxical precept "Never say never." An example of a reflexive question is afforded by "Are there meaningful questions formulated in English?" and a more complex case is the erotetic paradox of the coordinated pair of questions: (1) Is question two to be answered affirmatively? (2) Is question one to be answered negatively?

lett and Suber 1987.) This phenomenon is illustrated by such contentions as "This statement begins with a pronoun," or "All statements contain a noun." (Note that self-referential statements can be either particular or general.) In particular, assertions about assertion-in-general will be an example: "All meaningful assertions are either true or false," "All well-formed English sentences express a meaningful thought." Similarly, a range of discourse is self-referential whenever some part of this discourse falls into the range of its own discussion.

Reflexive discourse plays a particularly significant role in philosophy because philosophy is an inherently self-critical enterprise. One of the major concerns of philosophy is with the practice of philosophizing itself, and any and all deliberations about the significance, scope, and methodology of philosophical inquiry must be classified as philosophical issues. Philosophy (like intellectual history but unlike, say, chemistry) is one of the rare disciplines that are self-encompassing in the sense that methodological questions *about* the field automatically belong *within* the field itself.[2]

2. The qualification of "substantive" pays homage to the fact that various questions about philosophizing are *external* to the subject in appertaining to its personnel and their activities rather than its subject-matter materials. For example, deliberations regarding the psychopathology of philosophers, the organization of the profession, the teaching of the subject, and so on, clearly belong to other disciplines. Of course, *some* questions will fall on the substantive/external borderline in dealing with

As traditionally practiced, philosophical epistemology propounds universal theses regarding the conditions of assertability or maintainability of contentions: proceeding by way of assertions regarding all truths, all facts, all knowledge—in sum about all validly assertable contentions: "Whatever one can *know* to be so, must actually *be true*" is a case in point (seeing that, as Aristotle already insisted: "What is not so cannot be known" [*Anal. post.*, 71b26]). Evidently, all such unlimitedly universal claims about cognition at large will be self-inclusive and thus self-referential. Since they represent purported instances of knowledge, any universal feature of knowledge must hold for them as well. Such theses will, in the logical nature of things, be reflexively self-applicable; like the non-philosophical thesis "Properly formulated English sentences contain a verb," they must—if true—instantiate what they assert to obtain in general. But this self-referential aspect of philosophical inquiry has far-reaching ramifications.

2. Metaphilosophy as a Domain of Standardism

Philosophical inquiry is a critical discipline, seeking to establish limits and limitations—preoccu-

philosophical (rather than, say, sociological) reasons for the activity of philosophers—e.g., why philosophers only recently became interested in theorizing about literature or in environmental issues.

pied, that is, with the restrictions and qualifications that govern our human endeavors. However, particular difficulties arise when a statement (or more elaborate discourse) that is self-appertaining also happens to be of a limiting or negative tendency. If, for example, it is skeptically declared that nothing whatsoever can be validly maintained, then the thesis at issue is, all too plainly, inherently self-defeating. Or again, if it is a statement by a philosopher to the effect that everything that philosophers maintain is dubious and questionable, then it is clearly problematic in its tendency to saw off the very limb that is its support. Negative cognitive reflexivity is clearly self-threatening although, human knowledge being what it is, it is also to some extent unavoidable. And this circumstance has portentous implications.

We must confront the difficulty of combining three factors: universality, criticality, and reflexivity. Consider the following theses:

1. All contentions of type *T* are subject to some specified limit or limitation. (UNIVERSALITY + CRITICALLY)
2. Thesis (1) is itself a contention of type *T*. (REFLEXIVITY)

These propositions clearly have the consequence that thesis (1) will suffer from the negativity in question. Thus insofar as reflexivity and the criticality at issue are unavoidable, the only convenient option is to sacrifice strict universality, that is, to construe the generalizations at issue in a way that admits exceptions. This state of affairs has a particular bearing upon philosophy.

Reflexivity is unavoidable in philosophy. Clearly one cannot validate claims about philosophical standards from an entirely standard-free standpoint. Whatever we take as the working basis for our philosophizing can itself be questioned and will need to be discussed and legitimated in due course. We will eventually have to return to our starting point in order to assess, weight, and justify. The question "By what criterion or standard is a philosophical doctrine, be it metaphysical or epistemological or moral, to be deemed as superior to its rivals?" poses a supremely philosophical question. However, no philosophically useful standard of assessment can be extrinsic to philosophy and stand exempt from philosophy's critical evaluation. This matter of norms and standards of acceptability is not only a crucial part of the solution but an inevitable part of the problem as well.[3] Whenever and wherever we make a start at philosophical work, we have to take for granted some standard of

3. Even standardism's reliance on our experience of "the normal course of things" affords no Archimedean lever for philosophy, seeing that standardism itself is only one metaphilosophical alternative among others. That these others are inherently less satisfying is true enough, but only once we specify our requirements for adequacy, something that certainly allows for alternatives. (For the Kantian intent on "universality and necessity," standardism has little appeal.)

acceptability; we have to presuppose a given body of probative evaluation. But the deliberations we have to engage in are themselves philosophical ones: The standards of our philosophizing must themselves be products of our philosophizing.

Obviously, one's rationally adopted views in philosophy are bound to hinge on one's criteria for successful argumentation. But the reverse relationship also obtains. In philosophy, one's criteria for successful argumentation will also in part depend upon one's substantive views. One cannot evaluate the overall adequacy of a philosophical argument independently of assessing the acceptability of its consequences. Where argumentation takes us is always philosophically relevant; if it leads *ad absurdum*, then something is seriously amiss. Of course, philosophy itself is the proper judge of what is philosophically absurd. (What else can do the job for us?) Accordingly, reasoning from premises or assumptions, no matter how strict, can never constrain us in philosophy because if we do not like the philosophical conclusions at issue we can always find refuge in rejecting those premises. The plausibility of conclusions is always a relevant factor in the evaluation of philosophical arguments. We are trapped in a probative circle: The adequacy of our arguments hinges on the acceptability of their conclusions, and the acceptability of the conclusions hinges on the adequacy of our argumentation.

Philosophy is accordingly autonomous in that there is no extraphilosophical vantage point for assessing the acceptability of philosophical claims about the proper mission of philosophy and about the qualitative merits of work in the field. Substantive issues *about* the discipline must be resolved within the discipline, and the conditions that apply to philosophical contentions in general must accordingly apply here as well. (The limitation to *substantive* issues envisions a contrast with, for example, *managerial* issues such as how much funding the field deserves or how prominent a place it should have in the academic curriculum.) Philosophy is thus an inherently reflexive, self-encompassing enterprise, so that our general strictures about philosophical theses will also have to apply to themselves. Like "All philosophical theses must be asserted provisionally, subject to further clarification and qualification," the generalizations of metaphilosophy will be reflexively self-appertaining. For, if correct, any such thesis will also have to be self-applied. Reflexivity—to reemphasize—is unavoidable in philosophy, seeing that metaphilosophy is part and parcel of philosophy itself.

This circumstance issues a wide-open invitation to standardism on metaphilosophy, for metaphilosophy abounds in limit-indicating doctrines that are problematic in virtue of their reflexivity. Two examples are "Philosophical theses always belong to wider systemic contexts," and "In philosophy all of our universal generalizations stand in need of qualification." Their self-critical nature means that these contentions wear their anormality on their sleeves. But, fortunately, the standardistic approach to metaphilosophical generalization resolves the problems otherwise occasioned for such theories by the circumstance of their self-applicability. Once such generalizations are restricted to the range of *normal* cases the difficulties they seemingly cause can be seen as merely betokening the fact that they themselves do not belong to the range of ordinary and accustomed cases. Consider "Philosophical generalizations have exceptions." Construed universalistically, this thesis is clearly self-falsifying. But its standardistic construction averts these difficulties.

In sum, metaphilosophy's combination of universality and criticality paves the way to standardism in this domain. Reflexively critical generalizations clearly create problems when construed universalistically because of their unavoidable self-applicability. And standardism provides a natural and effective way of emerging from this difficulty.

3. The Self-Consistency of Philosophical Standardism

Interestingly, the fundamental thesis of philosophical standardism is itself a general philosophical thesis. Accordingly, "tenable philosophical generalizations obtain only standardistically" must itself be construed standardistically. Seeing that it falls within its own scope, it too has to be construed self-applicatively:

> Standardly, general philosophical theses are to be construed in the standardistic (rather than strictly universalistic) mode.

This contention, as we have seen, comes down to saying:

> Apart from certain exception-categories—certain families of "abnormal" or "exceptional" cases—general philosophical theses are to be construed in the standardistic (rather than strictly universalistic) mode.

However, when *this* universal thesis is construed standardistically, then any additional initial "standardly" qualifier simply becomes redundant, with its meaning fully absorbed into the text that follows. (The standardly standard is standard just as the normally normal is normal.) Accordingly, it is only in this qualified sense that the doctrine of philosophical standardism should itself be construed—that is, standardistically. And such a metaphilosophical position is perfectly self-compatible and self-consistent since on its basis various philosophical propositions can indeed be strictly universal without thereby automatically invalidating its strictures.

This possibility of, and indeed need for, the self-applicability of philosophical standardism is shown by the role of definitions in philosophical discourse, for some philosophical generalizations are simply definitions ("A *free* decision is one that results from the decider's own choices"). Clearly, the resulting conceptually mandated universals ("All free decisions involve choice in some way") need not, and indeed should not, be construed standardistically. But special situations of this sort create no obstacle to philosophical standardism which is, after all, a doctrine that must—in simple self-consistency—be taken on its own terms.

Then too there are *truisms* in various branches of philosophy. Thus in epistemology one finds (as we have seen) such unexceptionable generalizations as

"Only what is *true* can actually be known: If someone *knows* that *p*, then *p* is true."

Or, again, in ethics we have the unproblematic generalization:

"It is never permissible to inflict injury on others simply for your own amusement."

It is, after all, a moral truism that

- People should never be subjected to harm by others without good and sufficient reason.

- "Your own amusement" or "your own convenience" (and so on) do not qualify by themselves as morally sufficient reason for inflicting negativities on other people.

And these two ethical truisms suffice to underwrite the claim at issue. Such generalizations, which hold good on essentially *conceptual* grounds, must be accepted as strictly universal, and will thereby constitute a category of exceptions to the generalization "Philosophical generalizations are to be construed standardistically."

The occurrence of strict (exceptionless) generalizations of a definitional or truistic nature in any and every branch of the subject shows that philosophical standardism should be construed standardistically. But there is, of course, no good reason why the position should not be self-applied. On the contrary, one could (or should) expect philosophical standardism to be self-substantiating in exactly this sort of way.

4. The Range of Reason

It ought to be seen as unsurprising and only to be expected that the reflexivity-induced difficulties of combining universality and criticality that militate toward standardism in philosophy also operate within the broader range of human rationality in general. In reflecting on the human condition, one is strongly tempted to say things like:

- In human affairs, every rule has its exceptions: Here we cannot make unexceptionally rigorous generalizations.
- There are no secure "lessons of history": Every generalization based on historical experience has its exceptions.
- Every thesis and teaching characterizing the cognitive condition of the species reflects the intellectual limits of its exponents.

Of course, all such universal theses, however tempting and plausible-seeming, are at once in deep difficulty on grounds of mixing criticism with self-applicability. Each of them thereby wears the stigma of seeming self-invalidation.

However, such difficulties are swept aside if one views such limit-indicating generalizations from a standardistic perspective. When they are construed as holding in "normal" and "ordinary" cases, the difficulty at issue immediately evaporates as we open up the prospect that the generalization fails to conform to the general rule it stipulates. On a standardistic approach, such seemingly self-defeating critical generalizations are altogether unproblematic, seeing that each wears its nonconformity on its sleeves.

Rational reflection on human cognition is bound to be self-inclusive, with our deliberations about truth or knowledge or information, and so on, forming part and parcel of the pursuit of truth or knowledge or information itself. Many sectors of rationality's critical deliberations are self-encompassing and thus, in a way, circular. But nothing is inherently vitiating about such reflexivity, and it is certainly no ground for a skeptical abandonment of the inquiry. On the contrary, we would not want an account of our knowledge that did not itself qualify as part of our knowledge, and we would have no use for deliberations about rationality that were not themselves rational. To be successful in accomplishing its characteristic mission, our venture in human self-understanding has to be self-encompassing. The standardistic construction of the self-critical generalizations of the human sciences provides a convenient and straightforward route toward rendering them unproblematic and acceptable.

Philosophy's concern for the exploration of our cognitive limits and limitations unquestionably engenders problems and difficulties. But standardism offers a way out in providing for the circumstance that the rules we deploy in characterizing the phenomena of this domain will permit exceptions. In philosophical theorizing about human understanding, we are accordingly impelled toward a standardism which, by limiting the generality of its contentions, opens up the prospect of having the generalization at issue stand outside the scope of its own declarations. (Some of the difficulties that self-reference occasions for a wide spectrum of philosophical theories are illustrated in Bartlett 1988.) A standardistic approach affords our most promising pathway to critical but yet reflexive explanatory generalizations, though, to be sure, it does so at the cost of endowing those generalizations with standardism's saving indefiniteness.

EIGHT

The Problem with Far-Fetched Hypotheses in Philosophy

SYNOPSIS

(1) The fact-coordinated concepts of philosophy cannot survive a suspension of belief that abrogates the normality-envisioning facts—or purported facts—that provide for conditions under which alone such concepts are viable and meaningful. Accordingly, philosophical methodology has no realistic choice but to respect this circumstance of a factual involvement of its concepts. (2) The introduction of far-fetched, fact-contravening "science-fiction" hypotheses—a much-favored methodological recourse among contemporary philosophers—stretches our philosophical concepts beyond their natural limits by doing violence to the ways in which these concepts are fact-coordinated. Such a recourse to outlandish hypotheses is incapable of clarifying philosophical issues or of substantiating (or invalidating) the philosophical theses in which they are operative.

1. How Far-Fetched Hypotheses Pose Problems

Our concepts generally develop against the background of an understanding of how things work in the world (or better, are taken by us to work); they are tied to a view of the realities of nature and to the empirical detail of actually existing practices. Anyone genuinely concerned for the philosophical elucidation of concepts as we actually use them must accordingly bear in mind that the conceptual scheme that is their native habitat is not an abstract logicians' tool for dealing with the endless ramifications of an infinite spectrum of theoretical possibilities, but an historically developed product arising within the fact framework of a specific and concretely real cognitive setting. In consequence, these concepts are such that their viability is linked indissolubly to the experienced realities of this actual world.[1]

However, philosophy's interests being largely theoretical and abstract, the standards of precision, generality, exactness, and the like that are used by philosophers have traditionally been far higher than those of the practical people concerned with

1. Analytic philosophers have often stressed the empirically laden nature of our ordinary concepts, although they have done so from very different points of view (witness Wittgenstein, Carnap, and Quine). They have realized that this has substantially negative implications for conducting philosophy along traditional lines. However, they have drawn a dire and drastic conclusion from this state of affairs, namely, that the problems and projects of traditional philosophizing should be abandoned. The present far less radical prospect of construing philosophical generalizations in a more modest, standardistic way has not struck them, perhaps because their positivistic inclinations made them so eager to be rid of philosophical chaff that they are willing to discard the wheat as well.

everyday affairs. Accordingly, philosophers have generally looked upon language as imperfect and inadequate—in need of a thoroughgoing tidying up, clarification, and supplementation (if not outright replacement). But everyday concepts do not admit of this improvement without total revision, and thus without abandonment. They are made for everyday use and thus cannot survive unaltered in the more stressful atmosphere of theoretical concerns. In her endeavors to clarify them by well-intended hypotheses, the philosopher bent on theoretical tidiness will also distort and destroy them.

For the sake of an example, let us return to the situation of epistemology already considered. Ordinarily and standardly, the truth status of our claims to knowledge is coordinated with that of our grounds for making them. But the two will, on occasion, get out of joint. Sometimes, true beliefs are based on false grounds (as when Jones holds your Turkish miniature to be Islamic because he believes it to be Persian). Sometimes false beliefs are based on true grounds (as when Smith deems someone to be *X* because "She looks and speaks exactly like her," where the individual at issue is in fact *X*'s twin). Our actual conception of knowledge, which *coordinates* the truth of our beliefs with their adequate grounding, is viable as a meaningful unit only because these two factors are normally and standardly conjoined. To introduce hypotheses that force the two apart is not to make for the clarification of the conception at issue but for its annihilation.

Again, the contemporary literature of the philosophy of mind is full of robots whose communicative behavior is remarkably anthropoidal (are they "conscious" or not?) and of personality exchanges between people (which one is "the same person?"). But all such proceedings are intrinsically defective. The assumptions at issue call for the suppositional severing of what normally goes together, and do so in circumstances where the concepts we use are predicated upon a certain background of "normality." But supposedly clarificatory hypothesis should arbitrarily cut asunder what the basic facts of this world have joined together—at any rate, not where elucidating those concepts whose lifeblood is drawn from the source of fact is concerned. If we abrogate or abolish this factual framework by projecting some contrary-to-fact supposition, however well-intended to clarify the issues, we thereby destroy the undergirding basis that is essential to the applicability and viability of these concepts.

For another example, consider John Stuart Mill's critique of any theory of substance that contemplates a nonsensible *substrate* of sensation:

> If there be such a substratum, then suppose it is at this instant miraculously annihilated, and let the sensations continue in the same order. How would the *substratum*

be missed? By what signs should we be able to observe that its existence had been terminated? Should we not have as much reason to believe that it still existed as we now have? And if we should not then be warranted in believing it, how can we be so now? (Quoted in James 1890, 80)

Note that Mill's thought experiment turns on our supposing that "*it [the substratum] is . . . annihilated and . . . [the] sensations continue [unchanged and] in the same order.*" But this supposition is, on the face of it, absurd. If the nonsensible substrate of sensation indeed is what it is by hypothesis supposed to be in its very nature, namely, that which accounts for the substance and the ordering of our sensations, then the hypothesis we are being invited to make is simply self-contradictory: It makes no sense to suppose the phenomenon in the absence of that which by hypothesis produces it. (It would be like imagining the *sun*light in the absence of the sun.) If, as is indeed the case, our standard view of the world is de facto a causal one, so that our sensations are taken to have nonsensuous causes, then the prospect of discussing this nonsensuous causal basis without thereby annihilating its sensuous results is simply absurd—much like supposing that the oxygen and hydrogen be annihilated while leaving the water intact.

In philosophy, as in life, our experientially based concepts are inherently geared to the world's contingent structure, made into viably integrated units only by the factual arrangements of the world in which they evolved. These concepts represent internally diversified *combinations* of logically separable elements that are held together by the glue of a substantive view of the empirical facts. Every philosophically relevant conception has an inner complexity in which theoretically separable factors are conjoined in coordinated juxtaposition. But their integrity as viable conceptual units rests on a factual rather than theoretical basis: They hinge upon an empirically based, fact-oriented vision of how things work in the world. They lack the abstract integrity of purely theoretical coherence that alone could enable them to accommodate the demands of purely theoretical, fact-abstractive precision. When the very meaning of a concept presupposes certain facts, its explication and analysis clearly cannot, in the nature of the case, suppose that this basis is simply abrogated. The clarification of such concepts cannot be pressed beyond the cohesive force of the factual considerations that bind them into meaningful units and thereby underwrite their serviceability.

If we introduce fanciful hypotheses to abrogate these "underlying realities," then the foothold for our concepts dissolves and the relevant sector of our conceptual scheme simply dissolves with it. To say that no useful purpose whatsoever can be real ized in this way would be going a bit too far. (For example, a science-fiction style hypothesis can effectively bring to light the significant fact *that* certain of our concepts are indeed multicriterial and rest on certain empirical presuppositions.) But what this method certainly cannot do is serve as a basis for making our *existing* concepts more precise, because the supposedly superior conception that results in these circumstances will not—and in the nature of the case cannot—qualify any longer as a version of the concept with which we began.

This fact of an empirical background for our everyday-life conceptual scheme has far-reaching philosophical ramifications.

2. The Shipwreck of Conjectural Analysis in Philosophy

A widespread programmatic attitude toward philosophical inquiry accordingly demands reformation. Many practitioners of conceptual clarification assume a disdainful attitude toward "mere matters of fact." Seeing themselves as concerned with the abstract "logic of concepts" in a purely aprioristic manner, they are determined to uncover formal relationships that hold sub specie aeternitatis, and insist upon addressing conceptual issues in the abstract, independently of any and all factual considerations. But insofar as our portrayal of the philosophically pivotal role of fact-coordinating concepts has merit, this approach cannot be maintained. It becomes necessary to abandon the view—so prominent in some quarters—that one automatically ceases "to do philosophy" once one begins to take account of empirical considerations.

To be sure, some philosophers see the aim of the discipline in terms of an abstract exploration of theoretical possibilities. Along with Christian Wolff (who defined philosophy as the study of possibility as such), they take the line that natural science deals with the real world, while speculative philosophy deals with the realm of the possible. The present position is not totally at odds with such a view. It does, however, require one to heed the distinction between *realistic* possibilities that do not abrogate our understanding of the normal course of things and keep their speculative flights within the limits of the plausible and *fanciful* possibilities that kick over the traces of our understanding of the ways in which the world works. When we subject our normality-geared conceptions to the impact of suppositions of the latter sort, we jump into a vortex of conceptual chaos where we are utterly at a loss for what to say. Genuine conceptual innovation now becomes necessary, and there is no way of predicting its outcome. To the question "What would you say if . . . ?" we would in such cases have to reply, "We just cannot tell what we would say. . . . We'll just have to cross that bridge when we get there." For when we embark on a radical hypothesis that violates the conditions of normality, our normalcy-predicated concepts cannot be brought to bear at all. We have no ready answer to the question, "What would you say if . . . (if worst came to worst—e.g., if flowers started talking like people)?" When the hypothetical upheaval is so extreme, we are simply at a loss; we would have to go through the agonizingly innovative process of rebuilding part of our conceptual scheme from the ground up.

In the face of any counterfactual hypothesis, we have to "change the world," or at any rate some part of our picture of it. For every fact is surrounded by others in such a way as to block it in, so that changing it about requires changing many others as well. As a concrete example, consider the following belief-contravening supposition: "Assume that tigers were canines." Of course, this hypothesis, arises in a context in which, patently, we know each of the following:

1. Tigers are felines.
2. Tigers are not canines.
3. No felines are canines.

The assumption explicitly instructs us to drop item (2). But are we to alter the boundaries of the classification "felines" and so drop (1) as well, or to keep these boundaries the same and so countenance tigers as canines-cum-felines, thus dropping (3)? Obviously we must, in the interests of mere self-consistency, take one or the other of these steps if logical paradox is to be avoided. But of course the assumption by itself affords us no directions for effecting a choice. As this example illustrates, every belief-contravening hypothesis is by nature expansive in that its adoption always requires further adjustments. (See Rescher 1964.)

To effect the necessary readjustment of beliefs, we have only one guide: our grasp on the world's normal course of things. We want to create the least *possible* disturbance in the fabric of envisioned reality. But if the hypothesis at issue is sufficiently wild ("Suppose bees could speak English") then this guidance is lost to us. If normality is violated too radically, then we just do not have enough to go on in making sense of counterfactual hypotheses. When too much damage is done to the fabric of fact on which our concepts are predicated, then we literally "just don't know what to say."

If the interests of clarity and generality and precision (that is, in the interests of her theorizing concerns), the hypothesis-enchanted philosopher presses against the restraints imposed by the fact-coordinated concepts drawn from science and ordinary life—concepts with which her deliberations always ultimately deal. Seeking to separate in theory what mere contingency has joined together, the philosopher steps outside the restrictions of the real and endows our common concepts with a precision that is simply not in their nature.[2] All of our fact-coordinated concepts are predicated upon a certain background of normalcy and standardness, and when this background is abandoned through suppositions misguidedly intended to serve the interest of increasing precision, the result is in fact mere confusion. In striving for the theoretical tidiness of a generality that liberates us from commitment to contingent facts, philosophers all too often indulge in hypotheses so far-fetched as to destroy the very concepts being elucidated. Here, again, a standardistic approach is needed.

For the sake of an example, consider the rule which gives use of the classical sorites paradox (see Sainsbury 1988, chap. 2):

(**R**) When one adds but a single grain to a collection of sand grains that is not a heap, the result is not a heap.

Suppose we now adjoin the given fact, "A collection of three sand grains is not a heap." Then,

2. "Philosopher, c'est donner la raison des choses, ou du moins la chercher; car en tant qu'on se borne à voir et à rapporter ce qu'on voit, on n'est que historien" (Art. "Philosophie" of the great *Encyclopédie*, vol. 23, 342).

as the ancient skeptics observed, **R** leads us, step by inexorable step, to the now unavoidable conclusion, "A collection of a million sand grains is not a heap." Ordinarily, the contentions "*n* grains do not constitute a heap" and "*n* + 1 grains do not constitute a heap" stand and fall together. But we cannot, without paradox, maintain the rigid generalization that this is so always and invariably.

However, let us look at the issue from a different, standardistic vantage point. Confronted with fewer than around a dozen colocationally accumulated grains, we clearly are not dealing with a heap. When dealing with more than around fifty we clearly are dealing with a (small) heap. Over the range lying inbetween we are in a grey area where determining matters one way or the other is difficult. So the **R**-style generalization:

> Whenever *n* sand grains do not constitute a heap, neither will *n* + 1 do so

is a perfectly good standardistic generalization which holds good everywhere outside that exception category of the middle range from circa 12 to circa 50. (Note that no one has ever promised us that exception ranges must have sharply delineated boundaries. At this point a recourse to "fuzzy logic" has much to recommend it.)

One must recognize that the concepts we use in everyday life (a *heap* of sand, a *bald* head, and so on) are generally not so sharp edged that the rules which govern them, such as **R**, can be laid down with *rigid* universality and *strict* generality. But as one acknowledges that such rules can be construed standardistically, the paradox is at once averted. A standardism geared to the normal condition of things—to how they stand usually and ordinarily—can work wonders in averting puzzle and perplexity in the management of the vague and imprecise terminology that we make use of in the ordinary course of things.

For the sake of promoting clarity, philosophers often introduce distinctions that sunder what the contingent arrangements of this world (as we see them) have *in fact* conjoined. However, this produces not insight but problems. When we set facts aside, the concept at issue itself disintegrates in a destructive fission. And as we saw in the case of the *sorites* paradox, this disintegration generally manifests itself through an aporetic conflict of opposing arguments—all seemingly equally good but all, in the final analysis, equally unsatisfying (see also Rescher 1985). The language of everyday life is attuned to the prosaic, workaday practicalities of ordinary life and not to the requirements of theorizing philosophy. No matter how far we go in trying to explain, to specify, to qualify, we never manage to do more than to keep muddy waters astir. The processes of exposition never achieve the sought-for clarity. Problems, puzzles, and difficulties arise at every stage and, try as we will, they can never be eliminated altogether.

The inner stress among logically divergent factors in our fact-coordinated concepts is (generally) resolved only by the favorable cooperation of empirical circumstance; the tension is unproblematic because the facts (as we see them) are duly cooperative. But once we tidy up our reliance on these facts in the interests of theoretical neatness, the tension breaks out. The philosopher's "clarifications" by the use of extreme cases and fanciful science-fiction examples engender pressures that burst the bonds that hold our concepts together. When we set the facts aside and tinker with reality by far-fetched hypotheses, the difficulties crowd in upon us. Abrogation of the facts engenders paradox because the concepts at issue are geared to an implicit view of the nature of the real. Philosophy's tragic destiny is to be constrained to pursue the interests of abstract rationality by means of concepts designed to accommodate the facts of experience. It has to probe the merely possible with tools designed to handle the concretely actual, and address the necessary in the language of the contingent.

The traditional philosophers' quest for generality and precision has led them time and again to drive our concepts against the scalpel's edge of hypothetical cases that require sharp edged and clearly articulated resolutions to bring their contentual anatomy to view. (Thus Russell wrote, "A logical or philosophical theory may be tested by its capacity for dealing with puzzles, and it is a wholesome plan . . . to stock the mind with as many puzzles as possible, since these serve much the same purpose as is served by experiments in physical science" [1905, 484–85]. But this seems quite wrong. Experiments rub the theoreticians noses in reality; fanciful puzzle cases take us out of reality's domain.) This methodological recourse to puzzle cases is readily illustrated by the example of those extravagant hypotheses that give a kind of science-fiction aspect to much recent philosophizing with its proliferation of emotional robots, personality exchanges, and the like.

The lesson of these deliberations is clear. Instead of hankering after theoretical connections that obtain exceptionlessly in any and every possible world, the interests of philosophical inquiry are best served by an inquiry into what is normally or standardly true in the world in which we actually live. The fact-coordinated concepts we do and must use in philosophy cannot survive in the wake of a suspension of belief that abrogates a committment to the facts, or purported facts, that constitute the conditions under which alone such concepts are viable and meaningful. Philosophical methodology must respect such factual commitments. The introduction of the far-fetched, fact-contravening science-fiction suppositions—that much favored methodological resource among contemporary philosophers—stretches our philosophical concepts beyond their natural limits by ignoring the ways in which these concepts are fact-coordinated to the ordinary course of things.

The point of these observations is not to advocate an unbudging conservatism in the conceptual domain. Various advantages might conceivably be gained by giving up some of our concepts in favor of others. But the hermeneutical gain of elucidation and issue-clarification in philosophy is not among them. The fact is that to press our philosophical concepts beyond the limits of the realities that make them viable does not conduce to clarification but leads *ad absurdum*.

Philosophical deliberations ultimately pivot on untidy concepts attuned to our practical dealings in a complex world where some degree of oversimplification is always required in the interests of manageability.[3] In philosophy, we are constantly

3. "[Language embodies] the inherited experience and acumen of many generations of men. But then, that acumen has been concentrated primarily upon the practical business of life. If a distinction works well for practical purposes in ordinary life (no mean feat, for even ordinary life is full of hard cases), then there is sure to be something in it, it will not mark nothing; yet this is likely enough not to be the best way of arranging things if our interests are more extensive or intellectual than the ordinary" (Austin 1961, 133).

constrained to make rough-approximation statements—"promise breaking is morally wrong," for example—indulging in generalizations that eventually need further qualification and amendment since what is claimed is not strictly and unexceptionably so (here, in certain cases of incapacity or of conflicts of duty), but will at best represent how matters stand in the normal course of things. Standardism accepts a relaxation demanded by the fact that exact and rigidly universal generalizations cannot meet the needs of the situation.

A particularly important consequence of standardism is that on its basis the entire bizarre demonology of much contemporary philosophy can be averted. We no longer have to worry about cross-wired brains that share the same thoughts (or do they?) or shrewd aliens from outer space that can inspect our visual fields (will they "see the same things" even though their concepts are different?). In particular, once epistemology is viewed in a standardistic light, those various artificial-looking perplexities that befuddle its investigators simply drop off the agenda (or at any rate can be assigned a rather different and subordinate role). The explanatory pursuits of standardistic epistemology downgrade the significance of all those bizarre hypotheses and outlandish thought experiments dear to contemporary epistemologists. This alone is a not insignificant gain.

Standardism's normalistic gearing to the ordinary course of things accordingly has the great advantage of immunizing our philosophical theses and theories against the far-fetched hypotheses and bizarre counterexamples so popular among recent and contemporary philosophers. The methodology of projecting fanciful "possible worlds" and outlandish science-fiction situations is, in the final analysis, philosophically inappropriate. To force a concept into a mold shaped by hypothetical assumptions that simply abrogate its characteristic conditions of operation does not *clarify* this concept but rather *distorts* it. The result will not be a sharpening of one and the same concept, but an actually very different concept or set of concepts—one whose problems and issues we cannot resolve in the same terms. Such a distortion does not produce a *clarification* of the concepts in view but leads to their *abandonment;* it does not elucidate but rather abandons the concepts with which we began. While various considerations may conceivably warrant such an abandonment, the interests of the clarification of *existing* concepts cannot be among them. From the perspective of our standard framework of fact-presupposingly multicriterial concepts, the actual result of indulging in outré science-fiction suppositions and counterexamples will be confusion instead of clarity whenever some wild supposition abrogates the background understanding of how things normally work in the world that is an indispensable foundation for such concepts.[4] A standardist approach is far better attuned to the realities of the conceptual situation as we must come to grips with it in philosophy.

4. Thus W. V. Quine is surely right when he objects, "[In Schoemaker's discussion of Wiggins on personal identity] the reasoning veers off in familiar fashion into speculation on what we might say in absurd situations of cloning and transplanting. The method of science fiction has its uses in philosophy, but at points in the Schoemaker-Wiggins exchange and elsewhere I wonder whether the limits of the method are properly heeded. To seek what is 'logically required' for sameness of person under unprecedented conditions is to suggest that words have some logical force beyond what our past needs have invested them with" (1972, 490). Our present deliberations effectively serve to indicate just where "the limits of the method" lie.

NINE

Standardism in Empiricist Perspective

SYNOPSIS

(1) Since any conception of the usual course of things must unavoidably be geared to a background of experience, standardism represents a deeply empiricist position. The standardistic approach to philosophy sees the systemic conformity of our theories to the substance of our experience as one of the salient adequacy tests of our philosophical theorizing. (2) This makes for pluralism in philosophy. For insofar as people's experiences differ, empiricism will engender a variety of philosophical positions. Different backgrounds of experience equip different philosophers with different cognitive norms and standards—with different views as to what is normal and what anomalous, what is central and what peripheral, what is important and what unimportant. Such differences in cognitive evaluation make for different rational solutions to philosophical problems. (3) Such an experientially based pluralism is amply supported by our experience with the course of philosophy itself. (4) This approach does, however, constrain a lowering of expectations in philosophy. It means that we cannot expect the appeal of the philosophical views that we ourselves favor to be either universal (i.e., shared by all alike, irrespective of their experiential background) or necessary (i.e., rationally compelling for all intelligent minds,

irrespective of their particular cognitive-value orientation). Disagreement and conflict are accordingly bound to characterize the philosophical domain at large. (5) However, the variability of thought grounded in the variation of experience does not pave the way to philosophical skepticism. It is perfectly compatible with the idea of a "pursuit of the truth." (6) Empiricism involves a variability or contextuality that is nowise at odds with philosophical commitment, and does not degenerate into an indifferentist relativism.

1. Standardism Enjoins Empiricism

People's empirical—experientially shaped—view of the world unavoidably sets the problem stage for their philosophical deliberations. Insofar as a doctrinal position is articulated in terms of a conceptualized vision of "the normal and ordinary course of things"—as there is good reason to think that in natural and human affairs it must be—a philosophical standardism of cautiously interpreted generalizations is not only possible but appropriate. On standardism's approach, the adequacy test of our philosophical theorizing lies in the systemic conformity of our explanatory theories with the substance of our experience (where "experience" is not construed narrowly as observation alone, but is taken in its widest sense). Philosophical standardism thus represents an indelibly empiricist approach because any idea of the normal course of things is unavoidably linked to a background of experience.

Traditionally, philosophers have usually seen their task as a labor of pure reason and have held, with Spinoza, that it "is in the nature of reason to regard things not as contingent, but as necessary" (*Ethics,* II, 44). They have taken philosophy to be committed to necessitarian aspirations by its very nature as a venture in rational inquiry. But the very history of the discipline amply indicates that this position is altogether unavailing—that in philosophy, as elsewhere, reason without experience is blind. Once we accept this, and acknowledge that philosophizing too has an experiential dimension by virtue of which its deliverances become to some extent contingent and vulnerable to the cold winds of experiential change, we must also acknowledge that the deliverances of philosophy will not stand inviolate against the impact of circumstance but will be fragile and defeasible in the light of altered conditions. A philosophical doctrine must be flexible; it cannot stand fixed and unchanging but must, like all else that has life, learn to adapt—or else die.

People's views of *the* world is bound to be shaped by the nature of *their* world—the world of their experience. And just this is what determines their understanding of what is standard. It is, after all, the particular course of our experience of this world that determines what is important and what is incidental, what is central and what is peripheral, what is normal and what is anomalous. Our basic assessments and expectations regarding the nature of things emerge from the substance of our cognitive encounters with the world about us. The evaluative stance that people have—philosophers included—is for the most part shaped by the experiential flow of their interactions with reality. Rational people attune their beliefs, expectations, and cognitive inclinations to the course of experience. The best, and ultimately the only, availing test of our philosophical contentions is that of optimal systemization—of answering our philosophical question in ways that achieve the best overall rational systematization of our commitments in the light of the particular course of experience that comes our way. Here too, the smooth and efficient accommodation of our experience is the appropriate standard. And so, our theoretical positions in philosophy must be attuned to an appreciation of the empirical realities that emerge in the course of our experience. We must, accordingly, be prepared to accept philosophizing not as something absolute and fixed, but as something geared (in a potentially variable way) to the experiential background of its practitioners as mediated by the way in which they conceive of the facts and issues at their disposal.

To say that the concepts of philosophy have an empirical basis—and thus its teachings as well—does not, however, mean that they derive from a study of nature (as do the concepts and theories we deploy in natural science). Rather they arise through inquiries conducted within the setting of the cognizable phenomena that the circumstances of place and time put at a theoretician's disposal. They invoke deliberations conducted *in* (though not necessarily *of*) nature. The intellectual resources of people are as much defined by the conditions of their experience as are their material or their technological resources. The Greek theory of numbers thus reflects the limitations of intellectual instrumentalities—of cognitive technology—as much as the Greek theory of astronomy reflects the limitation of observational technology.

All the same, the conceptions of philosophy never manage to cut loose from our experientially grounded view of things. The ways in which we cognitively structure our experiences come to be reflected in the concepts by whose means philosophers set about their explanatory work. A Platonic *form* (or "idea") is geared to the world's natural or artificial thing-kinds. An Aristotelian telos is geared to the natural processes of developmental transformation that lead from eggs to chickens and from acorns to oak trees. A Leibnizian "law of nature" is geared to the principles of Newtonian physics. A Humean view of causation is grounded in the processes of an associationist psychology for which dispositions and tendencies are no more than conditioned expectations. All of the technical concepts of philosophy are introduced to account for the "established phenomena" that reflect a given culture's understanding of the world's putative facts as it sees them. Each and every such philosophical concept is empirical, not in the sense of being derived from observations, but in the sense of reflecting the world picture to which people have been led through the particular course of their experience. (The situation in natural science is not very dissimilar in this regard. Such dissimilarity as there is comes through the fact that in science it is not *understanding* within familiar categories that ultimately concerns us but *control* over nature.) In each case, the concept encapsulates a particular way of understanding the lay of the land regarding the phenomena at issue.

Yet if both scientific theories and philosophical doctrines are empirical and experience bound, then where is the difference between them? It lies principally in two considerations, the one relating to scope and the other to method. Scientific "experience" is always *observational*, be it in regard to natural or to artificially contrived ("experimental") situations. Philosophy construes experience more broadly to include two *affective* (emotional and evaluative) responses as well. As regards method, science appraises its theories by way of *predictions*. Philosophy, by contrast, does not endeavor to *predict* new phenomena but simply to *systematize* our beliefs in general. The salient flaw of a scientific theory is incorrect prediction; the salient flaw of a philosophical theory is inadequate systematization, that is, a failure to accord not simply with our *observations* but with our *convictions* in general. In philosophy we must construe "experience" broadly to include not merely observations but all manner of thinking, not only cognitive but affective as well. The "data" of philosophy go beyond the observational to encompass experience in general, its conceptual and evaluative ramifications included (compare Rescher 1993, chap. 3).

To be sure, the philosopher is, or ought to be, concerned not just with my course of experience or yours, but with all of ours. Philosophy is inherently boundless in scope and intention; properly speaking, its range of interests and concerns is unlimited. In philosophy, we do and must take into account also the ideas and theories of other times and places precisely because it is the *whole* of the experience of intelligent agents that is at issue. Philosophy's performance may be limited and parochial, but its intent—its mission—is invariably more ambitious.

2. Empiricism Engenders Pluralism

But is the normal course of things not itself a matter of standpoint and potential dispute? Is what is normal and typical not something that differently situated people can (and *must*) see differently? The answer in both cases is: *yes, indeed*. An appeal to normalcy can only carry conviction with those whose situation in the scheme of things enables them to see matters in this light. And there are bound to be matters that different people see differently precisely because their different bodies of experience present them with different emphases and different points of view.

Philosophers do not and will not agree on "first principles" because these are products that emerge from a mixture of nature and nurture, and life inevitably furnish people with different dispositions and situations, and thus with different courses of experience. What is a standard (or normal, or typical) feature in one person's body of experience may not be so in another's. Standardism accordingly invites pluralism. Since the philosophers at work in different cultural settings come equipped with different epistemic and evaluative priorities based on different backgrounds of experience, they also come equipped with different standards of appraisal and thus carry their reasonings from common premises to very different conclusions. Standardism *explains* rather than *denies* philosophical diversity, that is, pluralism.

We come at this juncture to a central issue in the substantiation of our present position. It pivots on the following objection put forward by a hypothetical critic:

> I agree with much of what you have said on the rational inevitability of dissensus and diversity. But you have failed to reckon with the crucial distinction between a consensus on matters of ground level *substance* and a consensus on matters of *procedure*. As you maintain, a rational acceptance process can indeed dispense with a substantive consensus regarding *what* is decided upon. But what it indispensably requires is a procedural agreement on modes of conflict resolution—a second-order consensus about *how* those first-order issues are to be decided. Consensus on particular acceptances is not rationally mandated, but consensus on procedural methods of acceptability determination is a requisite essential.

Despite its surface plausibility, even this more sophisticated argument for an at least procedural consensus is deeply problematic.

Their cognitive standards reflect people's sense of the plausible or bizarre, natural or outlandish, normal or weird, and thereby provide philosophers with the orienting perspective regarding "good argumentation" through which their position can be developed and consolidated. All these commitments and evaluations are shaped by the course of people's experiences, and experiences differ. Empiricism thus makes for a variation of cognitive perspectives; experience is too diversified and variegated in philosophically relevant situations to issue in a single scheme of cognitive values. No prospect of uniformity and consensus is possible. The biblical story of the Tower of Babel carries a far-reaching lesson. For better or worse, the prospect of homogeneous uniformity across the human scene is unattainable. Philosophers at work in different settings will almost certainly not reach a common answer to the question of the weight or authority of any particular sort of probative consideration, there being no inevitable and context-free way to determine unproblematically just how good our "good reasons" are.

No mind-set makes better sense in a rational inquirer—whether a scientist for a philosopher—than that of being *realistic* in the sense of keeping close to the realities of experience. To be sure, such a view of philosophizing clearly envisages a kind of enlarged empiricism. Traditional empiricists saw our knowledge of the world as ultimately rooted in *sensory* experience. The present pluralism sees our philosophizing as rooted in cognitive orientation that reflects a person-variable course of *ideational* experience. The variegated nature of philosophy, on such a view, reflects a pluralism of cognitive orientations shaped by the variant experience of individuals who operate in different conditions and circumstances.

Even where there is a consensus about process, there may nevertheless be sharp disagreement regarding matters of implementation. Even one single and fixed cognitive method (the "scientific method," say) will call for different resolutions on different evidential circumstances. But the problem deeper yet. It is simply false that procedural agreement is indispensable from the rational point of view. Where something as all-inclusive and synoptic as a philosophical position is at issue, one cannot sensibly maintain a neat separation between substance and method. Our substantive worldview is bound to shape and condition our inquiry methodology as well.

There is no escaping the fact that the issue of what constitutes a good philosophical argument is itself deeply controversial. It calls for elaboration in a way that invites diversity. How could absolute correctness be assessed? Clearly not *ab extra*: We have no direct, inquiry-independent access to the truth and so cannot validate a cognitive value orientation on the basis of its leading to appropriate philosophical theses. (The question of what theses merit acceptance is precisely what we use this orientation to resolve.) A value can only be substantiated (or criticized) from a vantage point that is itself a potentially disputable value position. The evaluative domain is self-enclosed and autonomous: There is no entryway into it from without. And just this paves the highroad to pluralism.

Even so, cannot such orientations themselves be (more or less) justified through rational deliberation? Though the correct answer here is "yes," this raises the immediate counterquestion, "But justification of what sort?" Clearly the justification must rest on cognitive values. We can indeed defend our cognitive-value position, but only from a vantage point that is itself value-laden. These cognitive-value doctrines are philosophical, and in philosophy every argument *for* a position is an argument *from* a position.

In philosophical contexts, there is no universal answer to the question or the weight or authority of any particular sort of probative consideration, no universal way to determine unproblematically just how good our "good reasons" are. The relevant evaluations reflect our sense of the plausible or bizarre, natural or outlandish, normal or weird. And these inclinations are inexorably shaped by the course of our experiences.

3. Some Evidential Considerations

Philosophical pluralism accordingly roots in empiricism through the interconnected operation of three circumstances:

- The endlessly variegated, chaotic nature of the world's processes engenders an inevitable variation in human experience: The complex and ever-changing variety of humanity's enmeshment in the world's affairs makes for ongoingly varied experiences.
- Variations in experience make for differences in cognitive values: Different experiences equip groups with different norms, principles, and standards of the normal, ordinary natural course of things.

- Differences in cognitive values make for differences in the conceptual mechanisms of problem resolution, and accordingly engender different theories, doctrines, and philosophies.

In view of these considerations, the linkage of empiricism to pluralism is only natural and to be expected. The fundamentally "empirical"—experience-geared—character of philosophical dialectic is what best accounts for philosophical diversity. It is only too clear that no rational Hegelian "inner logical dynamic" is at work in the history of philosophy, no inexorable rational exfoliation from abstract general principles whose general cause can be foreseen in advance—if only in its broad outlines. Not only must the substantive content of philosophical teachings await the historical development of the subject, but so must the very shape and structure of philosophy itself. The development of philosophy is patently not a matter of dialectical "logic" inherent in rational thought as such, but one of a process of historical evolution driven by the evolving course of science and intellectual culture that reflects the spatiotemporal unfolding of human experience. (No other consideration speaks as powerfully on behalf of an approach to philosophical issues in terms of standardistic/empiricist norms than does a critical look at the historical realities of the course of philosophy's own development.)

A standardistic approach to philosophy is committed to the idea that the systematic conformity of our theories with the structure of our experience is one of the salient adequacy tests of our philosophical theorizing. But does not such a position become trivialized through constituting a theory that is incapable of evidential validation and impervious to counterevidence? By no means!

One of the real merits of the empiricist approach that standardism represents lies in its ability to provide self-support—its success by its own experiential standards. The salient fact of the matter is that the pluralism engendered by a standardistic approach is amply supported by our experience with the course of philosophy itself. After all, the history of philosophy presents us all too clearly with a contingent course of developments that we can monitor experientially and then describe on the basis of whatever trends and tendencies we can make out with the wisdom of hindsight. The evolution of philosophy displays neither universality nor necessity but a complex course of contingent historical development whose patterns we can describe standardistically as characterizing the normal course of things. In understanding the nature of philosophy as in the practice of philosophy itself, it is our expectation-orienting experience with the observable realities that is—and has to be—our guide.

However, such a philosophical empiricism is of a nature that constrains a revolution of sinking expectations. It means that we cannot expect the appeal of our favored philosophical views to be rationally compelling for all intelligent minds, irrespective of their particular cognitive-value orientation. For it demands a deliberate departure from the long-established insistence on unqualified universality that has characterized the Western theoretical ideal of a science. But Aristotle was surely right. Perhaps we should not ask for more exactness than we can realistically hope to get in the particular domain of inquiry at issue. Perhaps we should, in the end, see philosophy as an empirical and experience-reflective discipline, and should—without endorsing the emptiness of skepticism—forego the traditional absolutistic quest for the necessary and the universal in philosophy.

4. Empiricism and the Price of Diminished Aspirations in Philosophy

Standardism looks to what is "standardly" the case, that is, to what our norms and standards are (or should be). It seeks to orient philosophical attention away from stipulative definitions and razor-edged criteria to the way in which terms and concepts function in their practical and workaday applications. It sees philosophy not as a would-be science but as a humanistic enterprise attuned to a more relaxed effort to understand the processes and to articulate the ideas inherent in our various intellectual and practical enterprises—a concern that pivots not on nature as such but on the resources and procedures of human thought (thought *about* nature included).

Philosophy as traditionally practiced has generally been characterized by absolutistic aspirations. Universality and necessity have almost always been the goal as philosophers have striven to develop their accounts in terms of principles that state how things are always and everywhere. But the very history of this project constitutes an ongoing series of illustrations of the futility of this sort of endeavor, and in the face of such failures standardism offers a healthy antidote to negativism.

Throughout the history of recent philosophy, negative views of the prospects of the discipline prevail. In reaction, many recent philosophers (especially in the Anglo-American orbit) have viewed philosophy as a kind of scientific enterprise and have accordingly set up certain methodological requirements—strict universality and rigorous precision in particular—as criteria both for defining and for resolving philosophical problems. Viewed from the angle of the philosophical tradition at large, the successes of this approach are limited and largely negative, laden more with useful lessons about what does not work than ones about what does.

Moreover, such a commitment to methodology has exerted a baneful influence on matters of substance. It has oriented the attention of philosophers to those peripheral and technical issues—largely relating to questions of logic and language—where such methods are more readily applicable, and has led philosophers to focus increasingly on matters of method rather than on the substantive issues. Their attention has been increasingly diverted away from the classical problems and traditional concerns of the discipline in a way that has produced a widespread disillusionment about the discipline even within the community of its practitioners.[1] But the fact is that philosophy has been frustrated by the self-inflicted imposition of unrealistic and unrealizable expectations.

Reacting to the patent obstacles in the way of satisfactorily establishing universal generalizations in matters of philosophical interest, many recent theorists advocate philosophy's abandonment (nihilism) or rejection (skepticism). Much of the history of modern philosophy from Kant to the logical positivists and the contemporary followers and successors of Heidegger and Wittgenstein has been

1. This phenomenon is manifested by the fact that the major movements in twentieth-century philosophy (logical positivism, Oxonian ordinary-language philosophy, French deconstructionism, and American scientism among them) all call for abandoning a concern with philosophy as previously constituted. The impact of such tendencies has produced a crisis of confidence in the philosophical community whose nature is indicated by the titles of such recent books as Cohen and Dascal's *The Institution of Philosophy: A Discipline in Crisis* (1989), Lübbe's *Wozu Philosophie?* (1978), and McCarthy's *The Crisis of Philosophy* (1990).

engaged in maintaining that traditional philosophy is embarked on a wild-goose chase and that the whole enterprise should therefore be renounced. Here, standardism can save the day. The facts of the situation admit of a far less nihilistic construction. It is not that we must abandon the traditional concern of philosophy to provide cogent answers to "the big questions," but rather that we should form a different and more modest conception of adequacy in this domain. One can and should be satisfied with answers grounded in generalizations that do not aspire to the classical goal of a strict universality and a necessity based on self-evident general principles, but instead rest content with a standardistic position geared to the normal course of things. On such a perspective, philosophy—its traditional absolutistic demands to the contrary notwithstanding—is viewed as an essentially empirical endeavor whose theorizing is content to accommodate the phenomena.

It is, accordingly, eminently sensible to adopt a view of philosophical theses and theories that accepts standardism's more modest and realistic manner. For such an empiricist approach frees our philosophizing at once from claiming a deeply problematic necessitarianism and from aspiring unrealistically to a degree of universality that is simply not attainable. Philosophy's mission and its method is now viewed in terms of resolving the big questions of the nature of the world of our place within it in a way that is concurrent and consonant with our experience. In philosophizing we doubtlessly try to make sense of *the world*, but we can only succeed in making sense of *the world as we "see," that is, conceptualize it*. We cannot ultimately avert the empiricist "fact of life" that our philosophizing has to be attuned to the conditions of our experience and is thus bound to reflect the scientific, intellectual, and cultural conditions within which it takes place. Philosophy differs from natural science both in its questions and in its methods at its disposal for answering them. In the final analysis it is just as experience bound as is science—just as tied to "the existing state of the art" in the linkage of its problem selections and solutions to the cognitive conditions of the day.

5. Is Experiential Pluralism Incompatible with "the Pursuit of the Truth"?

Yet what can be said to someone who offers the following line of objection against standardism's more prudently empiricist approach to philosophizing:

> A philosophy that proceeds on the basis of what is standardly (generally, normally) the case—rather than what necessarily *has* to be the case in the very nature of things—loses interest through its lack of ambition. To answer our questions in terms of what standardly is rather than of what necessarily must be is just not very satisfying.

To adopt this position is, in effect, to be unrealistic in holding that the best that one can have in the circumstances is just not good enough. There is a certain immaturity to this stance—a failure of good sense that ill befits the philosopher's traditional pretentions to a "love of wisdom."

But what does such an experiential pluralism mean for philosophy's search for "the real truth of the matter"? Is it perhaps a schizophrenic theory that there are as many realities as there are schools of thought, that whatever some perspective (or group) maintains as true *is* true, that there are as many realities as there are theories on the subject?

Experiential pluralism certainly does not expel the idea of a pursuit of truth from philosophy. It neither denies nor fragments truth and reality, but simply recognizes that every practitioner is bound to form her or his own view of it—that nobody has a direct line to the Recording Angel. It is wholly compatible with the view that there is such a thing as reality and that there can, in the final analysis, be but one correct doctrine of it. The theory does not endorse an "anything goes" methodology. Recognizing that others see some matter differently from ourselves need not daunt us in attachment to our own views of the matter. One has to recognize that only through perspectivally conditioned inquiry can we arrive at a tenable view of the truth of things.

In matters of philosophy, as of science, our only access to the truth is via the route of our opinions about it.

There is no conflict between our commitment to the truth as we see it and a recognition that the adoption of a variant experiential perspective leads others to see the truth differently. Given that we do indeed occupy our experiential perspective, we are bound to see *our* truth as *the* truth. But we nevertheless can and do recognize that others see the matter in a different light. The circumstance that different people regard its ramifications differently does not destroy or degrade the thing as such.

Quite to the contrary! A pluralism of distinct experiential perspectives is in fact also describable as orientational monism. It is not only compatible with but even demands an individual philosopher's dedication to a particular position. Such dedication need not be closed-mindedly *dogmatic*. One need not see one's position as final and definitive, as carved changelessly on stone tablets. As with our beliefs in matters of scientific inquiry, we can regard our position as the best that can be achieved in the prevailing state of experience and as subject to adjustment and emendation in the light of future developments—as correct only "in essentials" though perhaps not "in detail." (To *this* extent, the distinction between *our* truth and *the* truth can be maintained in this as in other matters.) After all, our only access to the truth about reality is through an inquiry geared to our position in the experiential scheme of things.

The tenor of these deliberations is, to all appearances, open to the objection:

> You characterize a philosopher's teachings as "empirical" in its pervasive dependence on the experience of its producer. But this is totally at variance with what philosophers generally *intend*. Their aim is not to provide answers that reflect a particular experiential point of view, but rather "to tell it as it is," to articulate God's own truth, as it were. And so your account is unfaithful to the enterprise as its practitioners actually practice it.

However, this plausible objection fails to recognize the profound divergence between *intention* and *accomplishment* that prevails throughout the cognitive domain.

The plain and unavoidable fact is that in inquiry, as elsewhere, we have to distinguish between aim and achievement. We may *intend* to assert the (real and genuine) truth, but all that we can ever actually *achieve* is to assert what *we think* the truth to be. "Tell me how it actually is, without taking the potentially problematic detour of discussing what *you think* it to be" is an absurd instruction.

The gap between intent and accomplishment is unbridgeable in philosophy. Its practitioners may well *intend* to articulate what is categorically and aperspectivally the case, but all we can ever *achieve* is to convey *how the matter looks* to us from the particular experiential perspective that we ourselves occupy. Even as we can depict the appearance of the world's material furnishings only from "where we stand" and not from nowhere-at-all or from everywhere-at-once, so we must describe the world's realities from a particular experiential point of view. (And such points of view come "only one to a customer.") Our intention in philosophizing may be altogether perspective-abstractive, but our *performance* is unavoidably and inevitably experience bound.

From the rational point of view, there is just no point in complaining about this. We simply have no alternative to taking "our own position" seriously (exactly because it really is—by hypothesis—our own position). To take it seriously is exactly to see it as representing our best-achievable effort at saying what "God's own truth" in the matter actually is.

Although the contrast between "the real truth" and "our present ideas about it" is perfectly sensible *in the abstract*, it is not something that we cannot possibly apply *concretely*. Similarly, the contrast between "our conceptual perspective" and "the right concept mechanism for thinking about the issues" is one that we can never implement in practice. To be rational, we must see our best-considered way of going at it to be the right one. But given that it indeed is our best-considered course, there is also no cogent reason to depart from it.

Only by asking for guarantees which, as a matter of fundamental principle, cannot possibly be had can we be discontent with the best-available resolution of our philosophical problems. (Even in science we can do no better than this, realizing that the practitioners of the year 3,000 will have a fundamentally different view of the issues from ourselves.) If we are to take our philosophizing seriously, we must approach it from the angle of the right and the true, as representing our best, rationally optimal effort at making responsible estimates in this direction. And this is a stance that we are certainly able, and perfectly entitled, to take. Diversity does not entail indifference.

6. Against Relativism

It is important at this stage to confront an objection to philosophical standardism that pivots on the charge of relativism:

> As the preceding discussion has acknowledged, standardism is an essentially contextualistic position, seeing that what is "normal" or "standard" depends on just exactly what the *accustomed course of experience* happens to be, which is clearly going to vary with time and place—with the historical and cultural context of those whose "course of experience" is at issue. In consequence, philosophical standardism is an open invitation to an endlessly variable and thus probatively indecisive relativism of equivalent alternatives.

The weight of this charge has to be absorbed and countered. The contextualism of which it speaks is indeed there: The "normal" and "standard" indeed are ineliminably empirical factors. We have no alternative but to concede that in philosophy as in science one cannot escape *evidential* limitation imposed by the observational and theoretical resources afforded by the state of the art of the time and place. But this consideration does not affect the nature and aspirations of these enterprises as such, nor engender an indifferentist relativism of equivalent alternatives.

Traditional relativism regards the choice among philosophical positions as rationally indifferent. However, a standardism that sees philosophical positions as inherent in the nature of experience renders philosophy not so much "relativistic" as contextualistic. Such a linkage to experience should not, and indeed cannot, be counted a valid objection to an empiricist conception of the philosophical enterprise any more than it could be counted a valid objection to the scientific enterprise. Quite on the contrary. Experience speaks for standardism rather than against it.

Granted its inevitability, the empiricist nature of philosophical standardism cannot invalidate this particular conception of philosophy. Rather we can and should acknowledge its experiential gearing as an unavoidable and inescapable feature of philosophy as such. A wide gulf separates an experiential pluralism from an indifferentist relativism.

Relativism, after all, goes beyond pluralism in maintaining that not only are distinct alternatives available but that they are equally good, each having as much merit as the others. The inherent defect of such an egalitarian stance is easy to discern. Perhaps, from the standpoint of the universe, all doctrinal positions are of equivalent merit, and perhaps they are all equal before God. But we cannot assume the prerogative of these mighty potencies. We can no more view philosophical issues with our minds without having a perspectival stance of our own than we can view material objects with our eyes without a particular standpoint. For us, who do in fact come equipped through experience with a particular philosophical perspective, only this one alternative can qualify as valid—the one that we actually have. If we did not see it as being uniquely valid, it would, for this very reason not actually be *our* point of view—contrary to hypothesis.

The step from a mere *pluralism* to an actual *relativism* can be taken only via an indifferentism that insists that there is really "nothing to choose" between that plurality of distinct positions. But, of course, a choice can in theory be made via mere inclination, conformity to fashion, or any of a score of such reason-indifferent approaches. The core of an authentic relativism lies in its insistence that there is no *rationally cogent* way of choosing. Taking this stance does, however, require a commitment to the idea that one can recognize a rationally cogent position when one sees one, that is, it demands an acknowledgement of rationality as such. But once this is conceded, then what price relativism? The position is deeply problematic and totters on the brink of incoherence.

Yet, does an experiential pluralism not put everyone's position on exactly the same plane? Well, yes and no. The doctrine does indeed see alternative philosophical positions as enjoying a parity of status from an *external* point of view; all responsibly developed positions are valid from a suitably favorable cognitive-value orientation and indefensible if we proceed from no orientation at all. But this externalized parity cannot be transmuted into a *deliberation-internal* argument against such positions; it cannot be made over into reason for not accepting them at all. Individuals do, in general, have an experientially engendered cognitive orientation and are able to resolve issues by its means. (The fact that words are meaningless until people endow them with meaning does not entail that they continue to be meaningless once they have done so.)

Accordingly, experiential pluralism as such does not entail a relativistic indifferentism. Even if we are pluralists and accept a wide variety of perspectives as being (abstractly speaking) "available," we still have no serious alternative to seeing our own rationally adopted stance as superior because of its very nature in being (*ex hypothesi*) the epistemic resource by whose means we transact our cognitive business. Faced with a variety of philosophical perspectives, the only rational—sensible and appropriate—course is to proceed on the basis of the one that in fact enjoys our allegiance for the sorts of reasons that we can and do accept as cogent.

Accordingly, the perspectival stance that philosophical positions can only be maintained relative to a particular experiential basis (perspective, orientation, or the like) accordingly does not prevent one from taking a dogmatically committal view of the truth—provided that one is prepared (as philosophers generally are) to see one's own perspectival approach as the appropriate one—even as in natural science we deem the cognitive position of our place and time as superior to that of all the *available* alternatives. And so, the variability of thought grounded in the variation of experience need not pave the way to a relativist indifferentism. Nothing about a perspectival pluralism constrains it to be at odds with philosophical commitment.

Our view of standards is inherent in and geared to the structure of our experience. The standards we set have no context-free theoretical rationale apart from this experiential basis. This is simply part of the human predicament; we have to go on from where we are. This consideration certainly does not delegitimate those standards. To be sure, there is no aprioristically privileged, strictly theoretical way to validate them. Their standing lies in their nature as experience-derivative standards: What vouches for them is exactly their rooting in our experience. And if someone else's experience sounds a different drumbeat, that is simply irrelevant for us: We ourselves "can't go back again" to be Galen or Newton. We must go on from where we are, with our own emplacement in the world's scheme of things. Neither nihilism nor indifferentism follows, but rather a perfectly cogent contextualism that faces up to the realities we actually confront. (Nihilism and indifferentist relativism are simply two more failed attempts to provide a theoretical critique of standards that themselves purport, very mistakenly, to have a standing and status outside the realm of experience-bound standards.)[2]

And no damage is done to philosophy by viewing the matter in this light. As long as we are *serious* about philosophical inquiry we must actually have a perspective of consideration of our own and take an evaluative position by assuming

2. But how is this task of standpoint-correlative optimization to be accomplished? This question has two aspects. If it is concrete *examples* that one wants, one should be able to find them in the substantive deliberations of any responsibly produced philosophical treatise (this one included); but if it is *theory* one wants—that is, an abstract account of the process of philosophizing in the face of diversity—then one must consult such metaphilosophical books as Rescher (1985).

a cognitive-value orientation. Here, "internally" from our own orientational vantage point, we ourselves cannot consider other positions as genuinely on a par with our own. As long as we have the courage of our convictions, as long as we stand committed to the cognitive values that undergird our philosophical position, only one resolution of a philosophical problem is in general optimal, and only one "appropriate" answer is available to serious inquirers in the existing circumstances and conditions of their labors.[3]

3. Some of the issues of this final chapter are dealt with at greater length in Rescher (1994).

BIBLIOGRAPHY
NAME INDEX

BIBLIOGRAPHY

Austin, J. L. 1961. *Philosophical Papers*. Oxford: Clarendon Press.

Bartlett, S. J. 1988. "Hoisted by Their Own Petard: Philosophical Positions That Self-Destruct." *Argumentation* 2: 221–32.

Bartlett, S. J., and P. Suber, eds. 1987. *Self-Reference: Reflections or Reflexivity*. Dordrecht: Reidel.

Carnap, R. 1962. *Logical Foundations of Probability*. 2d ed. Chicago: University of Chicago Press.

Cartwright, N. 1983. *How the Laws of Physics Lie*. Oxford: Clarendon Press.

Cohen, A., and M. Dascal, eds. 1989. *The Institution of Philosophy: A Discipline in Crisis*. La Salle, Ill.: Open Court.

Collingwood, R. G. 1933. *An Essay on Philosophical Method*. Oxford: Clarendon Press.

Davidson, D. 1973–1974. "On the Very Idea of a Conceptual Scheme." *Proceedings and Addresses of the American Philosophical Association* 47: 5–20.

Donagan, A. 1977. *The Theory of Morality*. Chicago: University of Chicago Press.

Dummett, M. 1978. *Truth and Other Enigmas*. Cambridge, Mass.: Harvard University Press.

Encyclopédie. 1770. Vol. 23. Paris.

Findlay, J. N. 1962. *Hegel: A Re-Examination*. Oxford: Clarendon Press.

Fischer, J. M. 1982. "Responsibility and Control." *The Journal of Philosophy* 79: 24–50.

Fodor, J. 1987. *Psychosemantics*. Cambridge, Mass.: The MIT Press.

Gettier, E. L. 1963. "Is Justified True Belief Knowledge?" *Analysis* 23: 121–23.

Helmer, O., and N. Rescher. 1959. "On the Epistemology of the Inexact Science." *Management Science* 6: 25–52.

Hempel, C. G. 1965. "Empiricist Criteria of Cognitive Significance: Problems and Changes." In *Aspects of Scientific Explanation and Other Essays in the Philosophy of Science*, pp. 101–19. New York: Free Press.

———. 1988. "Provisos: A Problem Concerning the Inferential Function of Scientific Theories." *Erkenntnis* 28: 147–64.

Hicks, J. 1983. *Classics and Moderns*. Vol. 3 of *Collected Essays in Economic Theory*. Cambridge, Mass.: Harvard University Press.

Hugley, P., and C. Sayward. 1983. "Can a Language Have Indenumerably Many Expressions?" *History and Philosophy of Logic* 4: 73–82.

James, W. 1890. *The Will to Believe and Other Essays in Pragmatic Philosophy.* New York: Longmans Green & Co.

Kant, I. 1785. *Foundations of the Metaphysics of Morals.* Riga.

———. [1787] 1965. *Critique of Pure Reason.* Translated by N. K. Smith. New York: St. Martin's Press.

La Mettrie, J. O. de. [1748] 1988. *Man a Machine.* La Salle, Ill.: Open Court.

Leibniz, G. W. 1875–1890. *Philosophische Schriften.* Vols. 1–7. Edited by C. I. Gerhardt. Berlin: Weidmann.

Lewis, C. I. 1947. *An Analysis of Knowledge and Valuation.* La Salle, Ill.: Open Court.

Lübbe, H., ed. 1978. *Wozu Philosophie?* Berlin: De Gruyter.

McCarthy, M. H. 1990. *The Crisis of Philosophy.* Albany: State University of New York Press.

Nagel, T. 1979. *Mortal Questions.* Cambridge, Mass.: Harvard University Press.

Nowak, L. 1980. *The Structure of Idealization.* Dordrecht: Reidel.

Quine, W. V. 1972. Review of *Identity and Individuation*, ed. M. K. Munitz. *The Journal of Philosophy* 69: 488–97.

Rescher, N. 1964. *Hypothetical Reasoning*. Amsterdam: North Holland.

———. 1982. *Empirical Inquiry*. Totowa, N.J.: Rowman & Littlefield.

———. 1985. *The Strife of Systems*. Pittsburgh: University of Pittsburgh Press.

———. 1989. *Cognitive Economy*. Pittsburgh: University of Pittsburgh Press.

———. 1990. *Human Interests*. Stanford: Stanford University Press.

———. 1991. *Baffling Phenomena*. Savage, M.D.: Rowman & Littlefield.

———. 1994. *Metaphilosophical Inquiries*. Princeton: Princeton University Press.

Richards, N. 1986. "Luck and Desert." *Mind* 95: 198–209.

Rorty, R., ed. 1967. *The Linguistic Turn*. Chicago: University of Chicago Press.

———. 1982. *Consequences of Pragmatism*. Minneapolis: University of Minnesota Press.

Roth, M. D., and L. Gallis. 1970. *Knowing: Essays in the Analysis of Knowledge*. New York: Random House.

Russell, B. 1905. "On Denoting." *Mind* 14: 484–85.

———. 1912. *The Problems of Philosophy*. London: Allen & Unwyn.

Sainsbury, R. M. 1988. *Paradoxes*. Cambridge: Cambridge University Press.

Salmon, W. C. 1989. *Four Decades of Scientific Explanation*. Minneapolis: University of Minnesota Press.

Shope, R. K. 1983. *The Analysis of Knowing*. Princeton: University of Princeton Press.

Sorenson, R. A. 1988. *Blindspots*. Oxford: Clarendon Press.

Strawson, P. F. 1950. "Truth." *Proceedings of the Aristotelian Society, Supplementary* 24: 96–118.

Williams, B. 1982. *Moral Luck*. Cambridge: Cambridge University Press.

Wittgenstein, L. 1953. *Philosophical Investigations*. Oxford: Blackwell.

NAME INDEX